THE RELATION
OF
THEORY TO PRACTICE
IN
PSYCHOTHERAPY

CURRENT CONCERNS IN CLINICAL PSYCHOLOGY II
*A series sponsored by the Department of Psychology
of the University of Iowa*

THE RELATION
OF
THEORY TO PRACTICE
IN
PSYCHOTHERAPY

EDITED BY
LEONARD D. ERON AND ROBERT CALLAHAN
University of Iowa

ALDINE PUBLISHING COMPANY
Chicago

Published 1969
Aldine Publishing Company
529 South Wabash
Chicago, Illinois 60605

Library of Congress Catalog Card Number 69-13705

Standard Book Number 202-26017

Designed by Chestnut House

PREFACE

THE FIRST VOLUME of this series dealt with a fundamental problem in the science of clinical psychology—how do you classify behaviors so that meaningful consistencies can be revealed and generalizations be derived. Not until behaviors are defined, classified, quantified, and ordered is it possible to develop theoretical notions about how specific behaviors are caused and ultimately how they can be changed. This second volume deals with the latter problem. Psychology has now amassed sufficient empirical data so that theories and laws of behavior can be formulated. Those theories of behavior we have have been tested primarily with lower animals. This restriction, however, has not prevented them from being extended to human behavior. Unfortunately, predictions from these theories to human behavior have not been uniformly successful, and we need not go into the myriad difficulties encountered in conducting behavioral research with human beings in order to explain these failures. The psychotherapy situation offers a more lifelike laboratory for testing theoretical formulations about behavior.

In the practical situation, however, we as clinicians cannot wait for the theories to be tested adequately. We have to make do with what is available. One of the contributors to this volume refers to this as "flying by the seat of your pants." But the techniques we use need not really be governed completely by trial and error. Over the years we have learned something about behavior and we do have theories (as yet inadequately tested to be sure) to account for some of the regularities. Specifically there are theories about psychotherapy and behavior change. It is the purpose of this second volume on CURRENT CONCERNS IN CLINICAL PSYCHOLOGY to examine how much psychological theory contributes to the day-to-day activity of the psychotherapist. Can the theories be applied in real-life interactions between therapist and client, and with what effect?

It is no coincidence that the second volume in this series deals with theoretical issues. The Department of Psychology of the University of Iowa has traditionally been identified with theory construction and theory testing. Whatever theoretical notions have been advanced have always had to meet the empirical test. We asked the contributors to this symposium to examine the theoretical biases from which they operate in the psychotherapy situation, and to explicate for us how their theory leads to specific behaviors on the part of the therapist and how these then cause the behavior of the patient to change.

In the first chapter Dr. Joseph Wolpe demonstrates the practice of behavior change stemming from classical Pavlovian conditioning. Dr. Hans Strupp in the second chapter takes a psychoanalytic point of view attempting to show how the behavior of the therapist can be consistent with that theoretical position. This view is further developed by Dr. Max Rosenbaum, who refers specifically to group psychoanalysis but incorporates many of the ideas and values of daseinsanaly-sis. In the fourth chapter Drs. Thomas Stampfl and Donald Levis explain implosive therapy, which embodies a model of avoidance conditioning and psychoanalytic formulations. Dr. Kiesler in a more eclectic vein than any of the preceding authors attempts to point out the gaps in our knowledge about relevant variables. The sixth chapter, written by the editors of this volume, is a critical overview and summary of the contributions of the members of this symposium. The last chapter is a report of the responses of the contributors to the editors' overview.

Thanks are due to the National Institute of Mental Health, which under Training Grant MH-5062 has made this annual series of lectures possible, and to Mrs. Jane Snow whose expert secretarial assistance has stood us in good stead.

L. D. E.
R. C.

CONTENTS

Contents

1

CONDITIONING:

THE BASIS OF MODERN

PSYCHOTHERAPY

JOSEPH WOLPE

THERAPY BASED ON the conditioning model is widely known as *behavior therapy* (Wolpe, 1958; Eysenck, 1960, 1965; Wolpe and Lazarus, 1966). Its methods are derived from experimentally established principles of learning. In recent years there has been a growing awareness of the potency of these methods in the treatment of certain categories of disturbed behavior, most notably the neuroses. Their application is mainly to those kinds of disturbed behavior that have their origin not in organic pathology, but in maladaptive habit formation. In behavior therapy a knowledge of the learning process is deliberately used to give the patient experiences through which undesirable habits may be unlearned.

To regard a neurosis as a habit is, of course, contrary to prevailing psychoanalytic conceptions. The psychoanalysts believe that the core of neurosis is a complex of ideas, whose painful content has caused them to be repressed into the "unconscious mind." They suppose neurotic manifestations to consist partly of distorted discharges from this repressed complex and partly of the effects of the forces of resistance that keep this complex repressed.

If this view were correct, behavior therapy—i.e., therapy which deals with habits—could never hope to eradicate a neurosis, because, obviously, the repressed complex would not be dealt with and the core of the neurosis would remain. Therefore there would be relapse and symptom substitution. Experience has shown nothing of the kind, even though some cases have now been followed for seventeen years. Occasionally symptoms do recur, but they are traceable to new learning experiences. They have not arisen on their own from the depths of the alleged unconscious.

Now a neurosis is a very special kind of habit. It is an emotional habit, and the most characteristic emotion is anxiety or fear. I use the word "fear" synonymously with the word anxiety. A word can always be defined as one wishes. If somebody else defines anxiety as fear that persists for a long time, or as fear whose cause is unknown, he is perfectly entitled to do that. I use the two words interchangeably because physiologically there is no difference between what is called fear and what is called anxiety. Although fear is most characteristic and most common, the reaction may take other forms— essentially variants of anxiety that the patient may describe as depression, or feelings of unreality. The experience may also be very strange and unfamiliar so that there are no words for it.

The crucial difference between normal anxiety and neurotic anxiety is that while stimuli in the former connote real danger, those in neurotic anxiety do not. It is normal to be afraid when confronted by a rattlesnake or the prospect of losing one's livelihood. It is neurotic to be afraid of walking downtown or entering a crowded living room.

Experimental work on animals has shown that neurotic behavior consists of emotional habits. If a cat is confined in a small space, it is possible to evoke what appears to be marked anxiety in him by painful stimulation with electric shock. When this stimulation is repeated several times, it is observed that the anxiety is evoked at a high level in the experimental situation even when the shock is not present. The animal will not touch food in the experimental cage even after a day or two of starvation. The reactions persist indefinitely without diminution even though the animal is never again shocked. It is important to note that these anxiety reactions are completely under the control of stimuli that were present when the cat was shocked. In other environments, for example, an open courtyard, the animal is entirely at ease. It experiences considerable anxiety in the laboratory that houses the experimental cage, although less in the laboratory proper than in the cage itself. It also experiences anxiety in other rooms insofar as they resemble the laboratory in physical characteristics. The phenomenon of transfer of responses to similar situations is a special case of stimulus generalization.

Human neuroses have the same basic features as those in the animal. Anxiety is usually their central manifestation. It is also often at the bottom of syndromes in which it is not immediately obvious, such as stuttering, impotence, asthma, compulsive behavior, or the so-called character neuroses. Most stutterers can speak fluently when they are alone. But they are anxious in the presence of other human beings, and it is this that interferes with the speech mechanism. Speaking to people without stuttering is restored if the neurotic anxiety response to people is deconditioned.

In most cases, a careful history reveals the anxiety to have been conditioned in highly disturbing experiences. As in the case of the animal neurosis, it may be an incident, a series of incidents, or a chronic situation. Specific aspects of the conditioning situation become triggers to anxiety responses and may retain this capacity indefinitely. It is also common for second order conditioning to occur; that is, for new stimuli to acquire an anxiety-evoking propensity because they happen to be impinging on the patient at the same time the anxiety is evoked by stimuli previously conditioned. For example, a young woman who had been conditioned to a fear of crowds was one day sitting in a half-empty movie house when it suddenly became filled with students. Her anxiety rose to a high level, providing a basis for the conditioning of a fear of movie houses. Human neuroses are like those developed in the laboratory in that they display stimulus generalization. When the young woman I mentioned developed her fear of movie houses, she also became afraid of other public enclosed spaces according to their similarity to movie houses.

Here we are, confronted with these very persistent and disturbing and incapacitating neurotic habits. And more exposure, mere re-experiencing of the situation concerned, does not lead to extinction, so we have the question of how these habits can be overcome?

Once again the answer has come from the experimental laboratory. The key observation was one I have mentioned: when cats were highly anxious their eating was inhibited. If the animals could somehow be made to eat in the presence of the anxiety-evoking stimuli, the anxiety might, reciprocally, be inhibited. Since several days of starvation did not produce a hunger drive strong enough to break through the effects of the anxiety, the next step was to attempt feeding under conditions of weaker anxiety.

When you shock an animal in an experimental cage, stimuli from the experimental room are also making impact upon it, and you get a direct conditioning of anxiety to these stimuli as well as the cage. This conditioning is weaker, presumably, because the room stimuli are more remote. Insofar as other rooms share some of the stimuli, they will arouse anxiety, but as they are not likely to share all the stimuli, they will arouse less anxiety than the experimental room. We put the animal into rooms with descending order of similarity to the experimental room, offering it food in each. In whatever room anxiety was not strong enough to inhibit eating, repeated portions of food led to a complete elimination of the anxiety, and then eating was found to be possible in the room next most like the experimental room. After a number of stages, the animal could at least be induced to eat in the experimental cage and thereby extinguished its anxiety responses there.

Techniques based on this principle of inhibiting anxiety by means of a response that can compete with it have subsequently been found to be widely effective in human neurosis. Feeding has sometimes been used in children's neuroses. Mary Cover Jones of the University of California was the first person to make use of the technique. As early as 1924 she helped overcome phobias by gradually approximating the object of fear to the eating child. More than a dozen other responses are also capable of inhibiting anxiety. I shall describe some of the commoner methods used for this purpose; and thereafter say a few words about methods based on other conditioning principles. It is quite usual for several anxiety inhibitors to be used with the same patient. The choice of anxiety inhibitor and the manner of its use are determined mainly on the basis of a thorough unraveling of the stimulus response history of the neurotic habit. I shall outline when and how three of the more common anxiety inhibitors are usually employed and give brief illustrative examples.

ASSERTIVE RESPONSES

The term assertive is applied to any behavior that gives overt expression to spontaneous and appropriate feelings other than anxiety. Expression of these feelings is instigated by the therapist when it is evident that interpersonal transactions evoke undue anxiety in the patient. In these cases it is found that the patient is simply unable to communicate what his needs and feelings are. The therapist may use various pressures to encourage him to express these feelings. Each time the patient does so, he inhibits anxiety to some extent and thus somewhat weakens the interpersonal anxiety response habit.

The feelings most commonly involved are anger and resentment, but anything from affection to revulsion may be relevant. A typical case was a 42-year-old married woman who was exceedingly diffident in all of her dealings with other people and who also complained of frequent tension headaches. When unfairly criticized, she would boil inwardly but say nothing. I impressed on her that she should try to externalize the resentments that she justly felt. The next day when a brother offered her some advice about the handling of a child, she advised him to keep his nose out of her affairs. This was the first of many acts of assertion toward him and others, whose result was that the anxieties which inhibited her behavior were gradually, and finally completely, overcome. With the subsiding of emotional tension her headaches came to an end.

SEXUAL RESPONSES

These, not unexpectedly, are chiefly of use for treating neurotic reactions conditioned to sexual situations. Impotence and premature ejaculation usually result from anxiety having been conditioned to aspects of sexual situations. The erection of the penis is subserved by the parasympathetic division of the autonomic nervous system and tends to be impaired by anxiety which is associated with activity of the sympathetic division. In most cases sexual feelings are preserved and the behavior therapist uses the responses underlying these feelings to inhibit anxiety reciprocally. In most cases of this kind, recovery in a matter of weeks is the rule if there is enough opportunity for carrying out the maneuvers prescribed.

When a man wrote to me from the Far East asking whether he should come here for behavioral treatment of premature ejaculation, I replied that it would be a good bet if he could double his investment and bring his wife with him. He brought her along and she cooperated very well. We began a program that required him to confine himself to the stage of sexual approach where anxiety was minimal, and to repeat that stage again and again until anxiety disappeared. Then he could go on to the next stage. This procedure implied that his wife had to refrain from pressing him to go further and from criticizing him if he failed to reach a particular standard of performance. It was in this that she cooperated so well, never goading him to go beyond a stage that he could comfortably accept. After five weeks of amorous efforts, his coital endurance had risen from five seconds to half an hour and his wife was having coital orgasms for the first time in twelve years of marriage.

Muscle Relaxation

This is an exceedingly convenient general means for reducing anxiety. It has autonomic accompaniments that are contrary to those of anxiety. Its main use in specific deconditioning is in relation to stimulus sources of anxiety to which no direct action on the part of the patient is relevant. For example, if a man is anxious in crowds, there is no kind of outward action that he can be advised to take to inhibit his anxiety. This is to be contrasted with the tactics required for the woman I mentioned who was unable to express herself; or for the man who because of anxiety is unable to ask somebody to repay some money that he has lent him. But if a person has a fear of crowds, or a fear of elevators, or a fear of rejection, there is no appropriate motor behavior that he can perform. He simply is oversensitive to stimuli of which he is a passive recipient. It is for this kind of sensitivity that one uses muscle relaxation.

The therapeutic use of muscle relaxation was first introduced by Edmund Jacobson, who required his patients to have from fifty to two-hundred sessions of training in relaxation with the intention of getting them to be as relaxed in all situations. Of course, "all situations" would include disturbing situations, and insofar as relaxation would inhibit anxiety it would tend to break anxiety habits. But this is a very cumbersome method.

Today, a more convenient technique called *systematic desensitization* is much more widely used. It requires only relatively cursory training in relaxation, spread over half a dozen sessions. During the same sessions, various situations belonging to an area (or areas) of disturbance are listed and then placed in rank order according to how much they disturb the patient. The ranked lists are called hierarchies.

The number of themes in a patient's hierarchy can vary from one to six and some patients have as many as fifteen hierarchies. Although many of these themes are of a kind that you associate with classical phobias, such as claustrophobia, others are not. You would not, for example, ordinarily class among phobias the fear of being rejected, or of being scrutinized, or the anxiety that occurs when there is implied devaluation of the self. You would not ordinarily call these phobic anxieties, yet the anxiety sources can be pinpointed and ranked according to their anxiety-arousing effect. Therefore, the way of handling them will be exactly the same as for a classical phobia. Incidentally, this is one of the reasons why "dynamic" therapists, presented with reports of behavior therapy, say, "We don't see cases like this. These are phobias and we hardly ever see phobias." Well, they probably do see just about the same range of cases, but they do not analyze them in this way. If they did, they would find that their cases also have antecedents to anxiety and acquire a phobia-like look. Actually, behavior therapists see many cases with a diagnosis like "character neurosis" that have been treated by psychoanalysts and are found to have the usual anxiety hierarchies when they undergo behavior therapy.

In constructing a hierarchy, situations are ranked in descending order according to their anxiety-arousing effect, i.e., the situations that are most anxiety arousing are at the top of the list. The items on the list are different from each other in a manner similar to a primary stimulus generalization continum. That is to say, a patient suffering from claustrophobia becomes more anxious the smaller the space, and the longer the time during which he is confined in the space. But it is possible that there are some items to which this principle does not apply. For example, a claustrophobic patient gives a high anxiety rating to having a tight ring on her finger. In this she is not physically confined. She also rates as extremely anxiety-producing the situation of nail polish on her finger. The point about these is that they produce the same kind of closed-in feelings as does actual confinement in space. And so they belong to this hierarchy on the basis of secondary generalization, and like other items, receive their rank order according to the relative amount of anxiety that they produce.

When the patient has been suitably trained in relaxation and when the hierarchies have been constructed, one is ready for the main desensitization procedure. The patient is made to sit in a comfortable armchair or lie on a couch. He is asked to close his eyes and the therapist says to him, "I'm going to ask you to imagine a number of scenes which in general you will do without disturbance. If, however, anything should disturb you, you will be able to signal this to me by raising your left index finger." Now, to take the patient with the claustrophobia hierarchy, the next step would be to present the bottom (i.e., weakest) item of the hierarchy. The therapist would say, "Imagine that you are sitting at home in the evening and reading the newspaper, and you see a headline, 'Coal miners trapped underground.' " After a few seconds he says, "Stop imagining the scene and relax. Let yourself go and think of nothing but your muscles." After ten or fifteen seconds, he asks the patient to imagine the same scene again, and so on. Usually, after the third presentation, he says to the patient, "If you had any disturbance at all to the last presentation of this scene raise your left index finger now. If you were not disturbed at all do nothing."

If the patient does not raise her finger, it means that there was no anxiety to the last presentation and then the therapist goes on to the next scene of the hierarchy. If she does raise her finger, the therapist asks for further information, "If the amount of disturbance has been decreasing from one presentation to the next do nothing. If it has not been decreasing, raise your finger." If she does not raise her finger, one can be sure that with a few more presentations of the scene, the anxiety will go down to zero. And then one goes on to the next scene. If, however, she does raise her finger, either the scene is too strong or the relaxation is insufficient. By this means the therapist makes his way up the hierarchy and there is in almost every case (with some variations in terms of lag) complete transfer of the deconditioning of the anxiety from the imaginary situation to the corresponding situation in reality.

In some cases, such as most of the classical phobias in their usual forms, desensitization may be a straightforward matter. In other cases, considerable skill is required of the therapist. To give you an example of this, I will describe an actual case that displays some of the complexities, even though I have to simplify it very considerably to present it in a short span of time. Mrs. A. aged 30, had for the past twelve years been afraid of going into crowds or public places like shops. She was also anxious when speaking to anyone other than her husband because involvement in conversation gave her a feeling of being tied down. Her neurosis had started following drinking at a party when she had become nauseated and was seized with a terrible dread that she might be seen vomiting. The fear of vomiting was itself related to an excessive concern about the opinions of other people. Immediate steps were taken to combat the latter by defining the limits of her reasonable rights and then showing her how to assert herself as described previously. The fears of public situations were not removed by this, and systematic desensitization was indicated. Mrs. A. was fearful of social situations even when she safeguarded herself against any possibility of vomiting by having her stomach empty. The more recent the meal, the more anxious she would be.

After training her in relaxation, I decided to "place" the desensitization to social scrutiny in a setting that allowed a great expansion. The first scene I asked her to imagine was walking down the center of an empty football stadium four hours after her last meal. She imagined this with comfort so at the next presentation I included one spectator. This aroused moderate anxiety. After three repetitions the anxiety disappeared. The number of spectators was then progressively increased over several sessions, at first one by one and later by greater and greater numbers until she was eventually able to imagine, without fear of being observed, about ten thousand people on either side of her. Next, I gradually decreased the time since her last meal at which she was imagining herself walking through the stadium, but we met resistance at one-and-a-quarter hours, because to her there was a real possibility of vomiting so soon after eating.

Treatment of the fear of being seen vomiting began with a request to imagine the printed word "vomit." Three presentations of this brought anxiety down to zero. Next she was asked to imagine a strange child vomiting one-hundred yards away. Anxiety was eliminated in four presentations of this scene, whereafter the distance could be decreased rather rapidly until at the end of the session she could comfortably imagine the child vomiting about three yards away. At the next session, the problem of Mrs. A.'s anxiety reaction to her own vomiting and nausea was considered with her. First, she visualized herself vomiting while alone in her own garden. A small degree of anxiety was reduced to zero in the course of two presentations. Next, spectators were introduced, first a single one at two-hundred yards, then increasing numbers at decreasing distances, until twenty people in the next door garden were watching her vomit five yards away. After this, she was put back into the stadium to vomit before an increasing number of spectators until the stadium was full. During treatment of the vomiting theme, which occupied about ten sessions over six weeks, Mrs. A. experienced an enormous lessening of her day-to-day anxiety. For the first time in more than twelve years she was able to go shopping and visiting, and to invite guests to her home without anxiety. The neurosis was finally entirely cured when some related reactions were similarly handled.

AVERSIVE CONDITIONING

A counterconditioning technique which is not applied to overcoming anxiety is aversive conditioning. It is used mainly in the treatment of various obsessional patterns of behavior. The chief agent is strong faradic stimulation to the forearm, which is much more satisfactory than drug-induced nausea because the time relations are more easily controlled. It has been effective in obsessional thinking, compulsive acts, and fetishism.

A modified technique for cases of homosexuality has recently been described by Feldman and McCulloch (1965). The essence of this technique is to present a homosexual figure on a screen and during this time apply a severe faradic stimulation to the patient's forearm. And then the picture is suddenly switched to an attractive female figure and the faradic shock immediately stopped. Thus, the female figure becomes conditioned stimulus for reducing anxiety while aversive conditioning is established toward the male figure. While this appears at present to be a considerable improvement on the use of pure aversive conditioning, I must say that it is not the treatment of first choice for homosexuality, because many cases of homosexuality, perhaps the majority of them, are based on neurotic interpersonal anxiety, which if removed the homosexual behavior often disappears entirely and is replaced by heterosexual behavior. Three examples of this type have been described by Stevenson and Wolpe (1960).

EXTINCTION

Certain techniques are based on "extinction," the breaking of a habit through the repeated evocation of a response without reinforcement. Dunlap (1932) introduced its use under the name of negative practice. It is employed in the treatment of such motor habits as tics. Through large numbers of voluntary evocations of the undesired movement, spontaneous evocations are progressively lessened.

This technique leads to a form of therapy described by different people in which anxiety is allegedly overcome on the basis of experimental extinction. The patient is kept in a situation that is *very* strongly anxiety arousing. (Dr. Stampfl's use of this method is presented in this volume in Chapter 5.) Its prototype was described by Guthrie in 1935. He treated a young girl's fear of automobiles by driving her through the streets of Seattle for about four hours. She became more and more anxious, reaching a state of panic, but then the anxiety subsided and subsequently she was found to have been freed of her fear. Such methods have also been described by Nicholas Malleson of London and by Victor Frankl (1960), the existentialist who uses the label "paradoxical intention."

There is no doubt that some cases can be cured by this sort of method, and sometimes very rapidly. But the situation at present appears to be that only some cases improve, some are not benefited, and others are made worse. I have deliberately used this technique in about eight cases, employing Malleson's variation of asking the patient to imagine the worst possible situation. One made an excellent recovery. A second one, whom I am treating now, has made significant progress. None of my other cases have benefited. In other contexts, I have found that exposing the patients to high intensities of anxiety stimulation can make them worse. It is really an uncertain measure, and I am not comfortable in using it. Another reason for caution about "high voltage" therapy is that its efficacy has never been shown experimentally. You can desensitize animal neuroses, but if you just put the animals into the situation where the disturbance is maximal, and keep them there for hours or days the anxiety level does not go down. This is not to say that deconditioning will never be effected by strong stimulation in animals, but we do not know what the potent factor is. My own belief is that this process is not at all a matter of extinction but probably the operation of what Pavlov called transmarginal or protective inhibition. If you increase the intensity of a stimulus, in some animals the response instead of reaching a certain level and staying there continues to decrease as stimulus intensity increases.

POSITIVE RECONDITIONING

While the elimination of unadaptive autonomic response habits is the usual focus of behavior therapy, there is very frequently also a need to form adaptive motor habits. Such conditioning is, as I have already pointed out, involved in the measures employed in assertive training. When the patient obeys your injunction to express his anger, he inhibits his anxiety and consequently weakens the anxiety habit. But at the same time, insofar as there are rewarding consequences, these reinforce the motor act; and the more the motor act is reinforced, the greater are the opportunities and occasions for the inhibition of anxiety related to the stimulus situation to occur. But motor habits often need to be changed even where anxiety is not involved. In treating nocturnal enuresis by the buzzer technique, the waking reaction is conditioned to the imminence of urination and this makes possible the subsequent development of conditioned inhibition of the urination that tends to occur during sleep.

In recent years, formal Skinnerian operant conditioning techniques have been used increasingly to remove and replace undesirable habits. At the University of Virginia, we treated two cases of *anorexia nervosa* by rewarding eating by permitting the use of a radio or receiving company, and withholding these rewards when the patient failed to eat. One of these two cases, a woman whose weight had fallen forty-seven pounds, has been reported in detail by Bachrach, Erwin, and Mohr (1965). Several varieties of psychotic behavior have been treated on the same principle, notably by Ayllon (1963), who has produced lasting changes in chronic schizophrenic patients, some of whom had been continuously hospitalized for decades. My own view of schizophrenia is that it is essentially a matter of biochemical abnormality, but even so, the schizophrenic does learn and he often learns very unsuitable habits. There is no reason why these habits cannot be unlearned. This is the sort of thing that Ayllon has accomplished.

RESULTS OF BEHAVIOR THERAPY

In contrast to providing merely an opportunity for transactions with the patient and hoping for therapeutic effects, the behavior therapist specifies how the undesirable reactions are to be eliminated. He can also sometimes state the quantitative relations to be expected between therapeutic operations and amount of habit change. In a study of desensitization of classical phobias (Wolpe, 1963) the number of scene presentations were correlated with the amount of progress toward the conquest of the phobia and a curve was derived approximating a simple power function.

To turn to statistical data, two fairly large studies by Wolpe and Lazarus (1966) have given the results of behavior therapy evaluating change using R. P. Knight's criteria: symptomatic improvement, increased productiveness, improved adjustment and pleasure in sex, improved interpersonal relationships, and ability to handle ordinary psychological conflicts and reasonable reality stresses. These two studies indicate that with behavior therapy the percentage of cases that recover or improve markedly is well over 80. The contrast that is most important is with the findings of the Fact Finding Committee of the American Psychoanalytic Association (Brody, 1962; Masserman, 1963). Taking those of their cases that were completely analyzed, the percentage recovered or much improved is 60, but, if you include all their cases, the rate goes down to 31 per cent. What is much more important than the relative percentages is the fact that the completely analyzed cases required something like seven-hundred treatment sessions on the average, whereas behavior therapy requires an average of about thirty sessions per patient.

How enduring are the behavior therapy results? The answer is that if the therapy is competently done, there is no relapse, nor is there "symptom substitution." Among a group of 45 patients followed up for 2 to 7 years there was only one possible relapse, regarded as relapsed because I discovered that he sought psychiatric therapy later elsewhere.

All the foregoing studies are uncontrolled. We need to

have comparative clinical studies in which matched or randomized patients are treated by different techniques. It is often assumed that in such studies psychoanalysis would show up to better advantage. It is as likely to show up worse. We simply do not know. However, we do already have several small-scale but very well defined controlled studies. Space does not permit a description of all of them, but I can mention one, a study by Gordon Paul (1966) at the University of Illinois. Using as subjects about ninety students with severe fears of public speaking, he got five therapists whose orientations ranged from Freud to Sullivan to take part in this study, paying them for their time as if they were treating private patients. Each therapist had to treat nine of these students with severe fear of public speaking—three by his own brand of insight therapy, three by a procedure of suggestion or support, called "attention-placebo," and three by systematic desensitization. Each patient had five sessions. In terms of the usual clinical evaluation of change—a combination of what the patient thought of his state and what the therapist thought —these analytically oriented therapists did much better, significantly better, with desensitization, than they did with their own insight therapy. I do not claim that this study, and the others that in general support its conclusions, are the last word. But it is an impressive indicator of the specific power of one conditioning technique and, to some extent, it is a vindication of the conditioning principle upon which this technique is based. It adds to the likelihood that in the next decade or so behavior therapy will become the standard approach to the treatment of neuroses and other learned disorders of behavior.

REFERENCES

Ayllon, T. Intensive treatment of psychotic behavior by stimulus satiation and food reinforcement. *Behavioral Research Theories*, 1963, 1, 53.

Bachrach, A. J., Erwin, W. J., and Mohr, J. P. The control of eating behavior in an anorexic by operant conditioning techniques. In L. Ullman and L. Krasner, (Eds.), *Case studies in behavior modification*. New York: Holt, Rinehart and Winston, 1965.

Brody, N. W. Prognosis and results of psychoanalysis. In J. H. Nodine and J. H. Moyer (Eds.), *Psychosomatic medicine*. Philadelphia: Lea and Febiger, 1962.

Dunlap, K. *Habits, their making and unmaking*. New York: Liveright, 1932.

Eysenck, H. J. *Behavior therapy and the neuroses*. New York: Pergamon Press, 1960.

Feldman, M. P., and MacCulloch, M. J. The application of anticipatory avoidance learning to the treatment of homosexuality. 1. Theory, technique and preliminary results. *Behavioral Research Theories*, 1965, 2, 165.

Frankl, V. Paradoxical intention: Logotherapeutic techniques. *American Journal of Psychotherapy*, 1960, 14, 520.

Guthrie, E. R. *The psychology of learning*. New York: Harper, 1935.

Jacobson, E. *Progressive relaxation*. Chicago: University of Chicago Press, 1938.

Masserman, J. H. Etiology, comparative dynamics and psychoanalytic research. In J. Scher (Ed.), *Theories of the mind*. New York: Free Press, 1963.

Paul, G. L. *Insight versus desensitization in psychotherapy: An experiment in anxiety reduction*. Stanford: Stanford University Press, 1966.

Stevenson, I., and Wolpe, J. Recovery from sexual deviations through overcoming nonsexual neurotic responses. *American Journal of Psychiatry*, 1960, 116, 737.

Wolpe, J. *Psychotherapy by reciprocal inhibition.* Stanford: Stanford University Press, 1958.

Wolpe, J. Quantitative relationships in the systematic desensitization of phobias. *American Journal of Psychiatry*, 1963, 119, 1062.

Wolpe, J., and Lazarus, A. A. *Behavior therapy techniques.* London: Pergamon Press, 1966.

2

PSYCHOANALYTIC

PSYCHOTHERAPY AND

RESEARCH

HANS H. STRUPP

I HAVE SET MYSELF the task of examining the current status of psychoanalytic psychotheraphy—with special emphasis on some of its challenges—and of reviewing some pertinent research bearing on contemporary clinical practice.

CURRENT STATUS OF
PSYCHOANALYTIC PSYCHOTHERAPY

The observer of the psychoanalytic scene who sets himself the task of discerning the current status and new developments suffers disadvantages comparable to those of the inter-

preter of contemporary history: he is too close to the events
and too much under their sway to view them in proper perspective. Personal biases and idiosyncrasies are bound to influence his evaluations and judgments, which must inevitably
also bear the stamp of his time. Seemingly significant advances
may in the larger perspective of the history of science prove
to be blind alleys; conversely, future advances may come
from today's unnoticed or neglected developments. We still
live under the shadow of Freud's revolutionary discoveries,
in relation to which contemporary developments seem rather
modest. This is not to denigrate the actual or potential importance of these innovations but merely to accentuate the
great theoretical and technical advances which have flowed
from such concepts as the dynamic unconscious, transference,
resistance, narcissism, and the like. The empirical cornerstones
on which the psychoanalytic edifice firmly rests have neither
been shaken nor replaced since Freud's time. History may
show that Freud's most basic and lasting contributions are
the basic conception of neurotic conflict and symptom formation and the contrivance of the psychoanalytic situation as
a laboratory for the microscopic study and therapeutic
modification of interpersonal and intrapsychic processes. This
includes most prominently the discovery, understanding, and
"handling" of transference phenomena. However, such judgments rightfully belong to future generations.

In summarizing principal problem areas which during the
last few decades have received the attention of clinicians and
researchers in psychotherapy, I would like to list the following:

1. There has been an increased emphasis on relating the
childhood roots of the patient's neurosis to his contemporary
functioning and adaptation, thereby rendering therapy a more
vivid and potentially deeper process. Past events of the pa-

tient's life are of no intrinsic interest to therapy except insofar as feelings surrounding them are still alive in the present and continue to have an adverse effect upon the patient's current functioning. The influence of ego psychology is particularly relevant.

2. Increasing attention is being paid to the personality of the therapist and the extent to which he succeeds in making therapy a significant experience for the patient. This interest is partly a function of a growing research interest, by sociologists and psychologists, in problems of two-person interaction in a variety of settings.

3. Intertwined with the foregoing has been the search for a briefer, more economical, and more effective way of treating patients. Attempts to regulate the length of therapy, frequency of visits, degree to which regression is fostered and the like should be mentioned. More radical departures from the analytic model are exemplified by experimentation in the areas of verbal conditioning and behavior therapy.

4. While indications for psychotherapy have become more inclusive, efforts have been made to arrive at better criteria for selecting patients for particular forms of therapy. This effort has as yet been neither systematic nor exhaustive.

5. The philosophical assumptions and theoretical formulations underlying psychoanalytic therapy have been questioned from many quarters and for different reasons, leading to more or less radical departures from the "basic model" advocated by Freud. The emergence of numerous competing systems of psychotherapy has probably contributed to the enrichment of the field as well as engendering confusion.

6. Advances in theory and research in sociology, anthropology, (linguistics, kinesics), experimental psychology (learning theory, operant conditioning), information theory, communication theory, the use of psychoactive drugs in psy-

chiatry, and in many other areas have been important but they are hard to assess. The development of group therapy, family therapy, therapy with children, and other forms of psychotherapy has had an impact on individual psychotherapy based on analytic principles. However, on the whole, these influences have led to comparatively few modifications or reformulations of basic psychoanalytic concepts and techniques. Two examples of challenge to psychoanalysis that have come from very different quarters are daseinsanalysis and behavior therapy.

Daseinsanalysis

This brand of therapy, which has enjoyed a certain popularity in America for some years, is a European import purporting "to combine the assumptions of existential philosophy about the nature of man with the phenomenological method, to achieve a more effective understanding and psychotherapeutic treatment of patients" (Ford & Urban, 1963, p. 445). To some extent, existential analysis represents a reaction to the naturalistic approach to psychotherapy implicit in psychoanalysis, which the proponents of existentialism consider inadequate for dealing with the "essential concerns" of man as a mortal and finite being. This view is pitted against a normative (nomothetic) approach, which has been the underlying philosophical assumption of psychoanalysis as well as scientific psychology based on the British empiricist tradition. Essentially, existential analysis is a viewpoint, not a system. Indeed, the very notion of system is anathema to its proponents.

The question of primary importance in the present context relates to the operations of psychotherapy, and the extent to which existential therapy differs from analytic psychotherapy. In this area one gets little help from the writings of the existentialists, although many case histories have been published. May (1958) has made a serious attempt to explain to American readers what the existentialists mean by "technique." "One might infer," Ford & Urban (1963) observe, "that they (the existentialists) have developed a new way of *thinking about* patients, but it does not lead them to *do anything different* in treatment" (p. 469).

"Existential analysis," May (1958) explains, "is a way of understanding human existence, and its representatives believe that one of the chief (if not *the* chief) blocks to the understanding of human beings in Western culture is precisely the overemphasis on technique, an overemphasis which goes along with the tendency to see the human being as an object to be calculated, managed, 'analyzed.' Our Western tendency has been to believe *that understanding follows technique;* if we get the right technique, then we can penetrate the riddle of the patient . . . . The existential approach holds the exact opposite; namely, that *technique follows understanding.* The central task and responsibility of the therapist is to seek to understand the patient as a being and as being-in-his world. All technical problems are subordinate to this understanding" (p. 77).

The role and function of the therapist are stated by May (1958) as follows: "The therapist is assumedly an expert; but, if he is not first of all a human being, his expertness will be irrelevant and quite possibly harmful" (p. 82). Without rejecting such concepts as transference, it "gets placed in the new context of *an event occurring in a real relationship between two people*" (p. 83). The term *encounter*, frequently used to describe this real relationship, has a mystical quality setting it apart from the prosaic concept of the ordinary human relationship. In other respects, too, daseinsanalysts charge psychoanalysis with a variety of flaws, of which the encouragement toward intellectualization and cognitive understanding, as opposed to true insight, is one. Daseinsanalysis stresses the now widely recognized truth that, " . . . the human being who is engaged in studying the natural phenomena is in a particular and significant relationship to the objects studied and he must make himself part of this equation. That is to say, the *subject*, man, can never be separated from the *object* which he observes" (p. 27). Existential analysis is intended to "heal" the subject–object split in Western thought.

In a real sense, the difference between existential analysis and psychoanalysis reduces itself to a schism between the European approach to psychology as a *Geiseswissenschaft* and the American approach to psychology as an empirical science. Yet the existentialists deny a lack of interest in the canons of science. They assert that their approach has its own method of investigation and that the frequently voiced counter charge of scientific inexactitude, mysticism, and a terminology that lacks precise meaning is a result of deficient understanding of the basic tenets of existentialism.

No doubt, the existentialist emphasis upon psychotherapy as a deeply personal and meaningful experience is well taken. The possibility that a system like psychoanalysis offers an invitation to substitute impersonal intellectual formulations about a patient for a human "encounter" cannot be dismissed lightly. Yet these shortcomings are not necessarily inherent in the system. By the same token, there is no guarantee that an unperceptive practitioner following the existentialist viewpoint can successfully avoid the danger of getting lost in the vagaries of a patient's idiosyncratic experience. Nor is it clear that the advancement of an empirical science is possible without efforts to organize the data of observation in terms of a coherent system.

To the person with esthetic, artistic, literary, philosophical, and humanistic interests, the existentialist position has a powerful appeal, particularly when viewed in contrast to the "empty organism" approach prevalent in much of American psychology, which impresses the existentialists as "human engineering" and "manipulation." The tradition of American technology demands that the therapist *do* something, "fix" something, or "set things right." On the other hand, being with another human being and sharing his experience suggests a meditative, passive approach, whose intrinsic therapeutic value has face validity, but whose superiority is as yet undemonstrated. Psychoanalysis, on the other hand, while having very different philosophical underpinnings than American behaviorism, also tends to view man as an "object" governed by psychic forces that can be objectively described and conceptualized. The battle between the competing positions is largely fought on philosophical grounds, and there are insuperable divergences in *Weltanschauungen* which are rooted in the culture and history of Western man. For these reasons it is all the more amazing that existentialist thinking has gained a foothold in American psychotherapy.

Still, when all is said and done, psychotherapy is not intended to take the place of a new faith, a philosophy of life. Nor is it a solace for the inescapable fact of man's mortality, his limited powers, and his susceptibility to existential suffering, loneliness, and anxiety. While firmly suported by humanistic values, analytic therapy *is* a technique for helping the patient to deal more effectively and adaptively with himself and others. What sets psychoanalysis apart from religion and philosophy is the attempt to discover and apply psychological principles and laws to problems in human living. In short, it aspires to become a scientific discipline. A patient, for example, who suffers in his interpersonal relationships because of destructive fantasies, often benefits from interpretation of his fantasies. This interpretation requires painstaking work, and the result is an achievement in which both patient and therapist share. Is this an "encounter"? Is there anything mystical about the relationship? To be sure, the relationship must be simply meaningful in a human sense, but there need be no pathos nor glorification of the "I–Thou." One may well agree with Sullivan's pragmatic dictum that much of psychotherapy is plain hard work. "Encounters" there may be, as well as occasional "peak experiences," but they appear to be the end result, the culmination of work in which resistances have been cleared away and the patient has become amenable to more direct, less defensive, and less complicated ways of relating to another human being. The therapist must possess empathy, but he also must have technical skill. The seeming paradox that the existential therapists do not do anything different in treatment than do other therapists may find its resolution in parsimonious formulations which hew as closely as possible to observable clinical data.

It must also be recognized that in all forms of psychotherapy the patient seems to acquire a conviction, a faith, or a system of beliefs that sustains him in the struggle against his neurotic trends and his relationships with other people and the environment at large. The essence of this faith is difficult to define and may take multiple forms. It may express itself as a sense of trust in the benevolence of a superior being (a personal God); a conviction of the strength of one's own powers, a belief that one can master adversity. It may also express itself in an ability to cope with the vicissitudes of life, and the ability to retain a sense of integrity and wholeness, a conviction of the truth of a set of scientific principles. All of this may express the fact that *one is not alone in a hostile world*. The root for this faith may lie in the patient's identification with the therapist, which in turn is based upon the child's trust in his parents (seen by Freud as the prototype of the Judeo-Christian belief in God as a Good Father). Trust, belief in the essential goodness and protective powers of another person, and love with its counterpart, humility (as opposed to narcissism), appear to be essential components of a person's ego strength. It is difficult to see how any form of psychotherapy can be successful which fails to mediate these qualities through the patient's relationship with the therapist. As noted, we are as yet unclear about *how* this process succeeds in producing therapeutic change—terms like identification and introjection do not really explain it—but observation shows that it does happen. The task for research is to spell out the conditions, thus insuring a greater likelihood of their occurrence. This sets psychotherapy apart from religion and other forms of psychological influence. It is apparent, however, that the major world religions have a long priority in their recognition of the overriding importance of what for lack of a better term may be called *basic trust*.

Behavior Therapy

This development offers a second challenge to analytic therapy from a group of scientists who avow a "hard-nosed" approach to psychotherapy. Their banner, "behavior modification," refers to techniques which are broadly related to the field of learning, "but learning with a particular intent, namely clinical treatment and change" (Watson, 1962, p. 19). The emphasis of these approaches rests on behavior. To quote Ullman & Krasner (1965): "The working behavior therapist is likely to ask three question: (a) what behavior is maladaptive, that is, what subject behaviors should be increased or decreased; (b) what environmental contingencies *currently* support the subject's behavior (either to maintain his undesirable behavior or to reduce the likelihood of his performing a more adaptive response); and (c) what environmental changes, usually reinforcing stimuli, may be manipulated to alter the subject's behavior" (p. 1-2).

Historically, behavior modification has its roots in the experimental work of Pavlov on the conditioned response, in learning theory as developed within American psychology, and in the behaviorism of John B. Watson. Clinical applications have been spearheaded by Dollard and Miller, Eysenck, Mowrer, Wolpe, and the followers of Skinner. A vast literature attests to the viability and popularity of the approach within American and British psychology (Krasner & Ullman, 1965, and Ullman & Krasner, 1965). The appeal to academic psychologists is supported by the focus of behavior therapists on experimentation, empirical proof, and the use of concepts that make a minimum of theoretical assumptions. The proponents believe these tenets are continually ignored by psychoanalytic therapists of whom behavior therapists as a group are highly critical. The attack on the uselessness of intrapsychic variables is epitomized by Eysenck (1959): "Learning theory does not postulate . . . 'unconscious causes,' but regards neurotic symptoms as simple learned habits; there is no neurosis underlying the symptom, but merely the symptom itself. *Get rid of the symptom and you have eliminated neurosis.*"

Behavior modification, therefore, is aimed at elimination or modification of the maladaptive response itself, which is considered the problem to which the therapist should address himself. Contrary to psychoanalytic therapy, which views any behavioral act as a complex, overdetermined resultant of motivational forces, behavior therapy rejects all intrapsychic determinants hypothesized by analytic therapy. Neurotic symptoms thus are seen as habits which are more or less fortuitously learned without subserving important motivational functions for the individual. Psychoanalytic psychology asserts that a symptom is merely a surface manifestation of an underlying intrapsychic conflict, which fulfills an important although abortive function in the individual's adaptation. The suppression or modification of the symptom without change in the underlying psychic structure should lead to the substitution of another neurotic symptom. Citing experimental results, behavior therapists assert that symptom substitution rarely occurs, and they consider it of little consequence. The psychoanalytic model of symptom formation is often regarded by behavior therapists as a "medical model" (supposedly because it postulates underlying causes). The behavior therapy model is extolled as a "psychological" one. Without getting involved in semantics, a rather convincing case can be made that the psychoanalytic theory of neurosis, insofar as it is based on purely psychological concepts, is as much a "psychological" theory as a theory based on conditioning principles.

In any event, behavior therapists have attacked psychoanalytic therapy on account of its inordinate length, expense, its narrow range of applicability, and, above all, its alleged ineffectiveness. Beginning with Eysenck's (1952) article questioning the effectiveness of psychoanalytic therapy, increasingly bolder claims have been advanced (Wolpe, 1958; Eysenck, 1961) for the superiority of behavior therapy, particularly in the treatment of phobias, but more recently also in modifying many other conditions. In view of the difficulty of providing adequate experimental controls, the fluidity of outcome criteria and their consequent noncomparability, the issue, despite the zeal of the behavior therapists, must be considered unsettled at the present time. The fact that a given technique "works" in particular instances does not necessarily prove the superiority of the underlying theoretical system: all systems of psychotherapy can point to successes as well as failures. Furthermore, the measurement of psychological change is as yet so tenuous that meaningful comparisons in terms of percentage improvement are untrustworthy and have little more than propagandistic value.

To the credit of the behavior therapists, it must be said that their insistence on empirical indicators, their critical scrutiny of concepts that resist validation by scientific methods, matched by any comparable effort on the side of analytically and their eagerness to experiment with novel techniques is unoriented investigators. The utter simplicity of the approach, too, has an enormous appeal.

Behavior therapists maintain that analytically oriented therapists, too, employ reinforcement principles albeit in an unsystematic way, and that there are common elements in all forms of psychotherapy. Both of these assertions are probably true. For example, the analytically oriented therapist tends to "reward" patients through more active verbal participation and interpretations when they are working on their problems in nondefensive ways, whereas resistance is "punished" by the therapist's silence. A common element in all approaches is probably the therapist's interest, dedication, and conviction of the "truth" of his theories. For example, Marmor (1962) calls attention to the self-validating character of therapeutic theories.

By the same token, analytic therapists use the same argument ("My opponent does the same thing I do, only less effectively or in an inferior manner") by pointing out that the "indoctrination" of patients in behavior therapy achieves its success largely through a crass exploitation of the transference relationship. They also cite historical evidence to show that, for example, persuading patients to expose themselves to phobically avoided situations is an old technique.

One of the most impressive criticisms of behavior modification is its simplistic view of human behavior and neurosis. It has little to say about complex problems such as neurotic depressions, obsessive-compulsive disorders, character problems, and the wide range of difficulties in living which patients typically present to the therapist, in addition to specific neurotic symptoms (like phobias). The number of patients who complain of isolated neurotic symptoms, as any clinician can testify, is exceedingly small. On the other hand, behavior therapists have pioneered in treating patients whose intellectual and personality resources usually make them unsuitable candidates for analytic therapy, which clearly places a premium on the patient's ability to verbalize, to enter into a collaborative relationship with a therapist, and to immerse himself in the "as if" relationship of the transference.

The argument of objectivity, scientism, and the "proven principles" of learning theory, with which behavior therapists buttress the claims of superiority for their position, has recently been challenged from an unexpected source—by psychologists versed in learning theory (Breger and McGaugh, 1965). Characterizing the behavior therapist's position as "untenable" (p. 340), these authors adduce evidence to show that learning theory principles are not nearly as well established as the behavior therapists maintain. They conclude that "there seems to be enough question about what goes on in verbal conditioning itself to indicate that it cannot be utilized as a more basic explanation for complex phenomena such as psychotherapy" (p. 346). Furthermore, "Wolpe's case histories are classic testaments to the fact that he cannot, and does not, apply the symptom approach when working with actual data" (p. 350). Breger and McGaugh argue that the phenomena of neurosis do not fit a symptom or response theory and that intrapsychic variables are a more adequate way of conceptualizing neurotic disturbances. They state:

To sum it up, it would seem that the behaviorists have reached a position where an inadequate conceptual framework forces them to adopt an inadequate and superficial view of the very data that they are concerned with. They are then forced to slip many of the key facts in the back door, so to speak, for example, when all sorts of fantasy, imaginary, and thought processes are blithely called responses" (p. 350).

The therapeutic effectiveness of a system, even if it could be convincingly demonstrated, which at present seems impossible, remains but one criterion by which to judge its value. Perhaps a more important one is its actual and potential explanatory value to account for the major phenomena within its domain. In this realm, I believe, psychoanalytic theory has no serious contender.

Conclusion on Current Status of Psychoanalytic Therapy

In critically assessing the current status of psychoanalytic therapy one cannot fail to record a certain disappointment with the achievements and promise of this method of therapy. While continuing to occupy a position of high prestige in the United States, psychoanalysis has sustained a loss in scientific status. This conclusion emerges despite the fact that the last few decades have witnessed the emergence of research studies dealing with aspects of the *general* theory of psychoanalysis.

Furthermore, there has been an unprecedented increase in the number of therapists whose training has been deeply influenced by Freudian principles, which in more or less diluted form make up the core of the "psychodynamic viewpoint." The steady rise in the number of therapists has been a result of the momentous growth of clinical psychology, psychiatric social work, and psychiatry. Graduates of these training programs, under the impact of the enormous social need for their services, have broadened their activities to include brief psychotherapy, group therapy, family therapy, and numerous other variants. In this connection, a fair amount of informal experimentation has occurred. Many therapists who have been trained in "orthodox" psychoanalysis appear to treat sizable numbers of patients by forms of psychotherapy other than strict psychoanalysis. Additionally, there has been a growing awareness of the necessity to tailor psychotherapy to the needs of an ever expanding patient population, many of whose members do not meet the rigorous criteria originally postulated for psychoanalytic treatment.

Contrary to a trend of the 1940's, when psychoanalysis was considered the panacea for virtually all of modern man's ills and the "royal road" to the solution of difficulties in living, there is now a reluctance on the part of both patients and therapists to engage in long-term intensive treatment over the years. Analyses lasting six, eight, or even ten years were at one time not uncommon but are apparently becoming rarer. This is not to deny the need for intensive therapy in certain cases, but therapists also realize that psychotherapy eventually reaches a point of diminishing returns, beyond which further therapy becomes inexpedient if not positively harmful. However, in the absence of conclusive research, only broad clinical indicators are available to guide the therapist in determining this juncture.

Although there continue to be heard the strident voices of caustic critics who would dismiss the value of psychoanalytic therapy altogether, there seems little question that patients do improve and that they benefit from psychoanalytic therapy carried on over an extended period of time. Clinical experience amply documents the value of psychoanalysis and psychotherapy based on psychoanalytic principles with a variety of patients. This assertion seems warranted despite the absence of ironclad criteria by which to measure the effectiveness of therapy. However, other forms of psychotherapy can point to comparable successes, and the superiority of any method of therapy remains a moot question.[1] There are no reliable criteria for differentiating "structural changes in the ego" from "transference cures," nor can we as yet explain, except on a post hoc basis, why the outcomes of therapy are sometimes impressive and at other times disappointing.

Among additional factors accounting for the lessening enthusiasm for psychoanalytic therapy is the absence of incisive advances in the technology of psychotherapy during the last quarter of a century. This lack of progress beyond Freud's discoveries is particularly striking in comparison with rapid developments in such fields as psychopharmacology, genetics, and psychophysiology—to name but a few. I shall not consider whether such comparisons are relevant or justified. The fact remains that with the increasing recognition of the mental health problem by government bodies and the public at large, the demand for efficient, inexpensive, and "easy" solutions has received a great impetus. In contrast, it is alleged in various quarters that psychoanalytic therapy has

---

[1] I cannot take seriously Eysenck's contention that a large proportion of patients with serious neurotic problems in living "spontaneously improve" within one to two years of "onset." Such a statement is simply at variance with clinical observation.

failed to answer the challenge, and—what amounts to a more serious charge—has blithely ignored its existence. The accusation has been made that, instead of objectively examining its premises and systematically studying its operations in collaboration with cognate sciences, psychotherapy (and, particularly, organized psychoanalysis) has withdrawn to an ivory tower, from which it contemplates increasingly esoteric problems without paying attention to the societal problems which urgently demand solution.

These feelings of dissatisfaction are voiced not only by unsympathetic or uninformed critics, but also by prominent therapists and theoreticians whose extensive training and experience command respect. It will not do to call their strictures "unresolved transferences" or worse. It must also be recognized that the psychoanalytic *mystique* (Glover's term) has exerted an untoward influence on the free development of the field. The close alliance of organized psychoanalysis with psychiatry and medicine, the likelihood of whose occurrence Freud already viewed with foreboding (see Szasz, 1961; Eissler, 1965) and the guild character of organized psychoanalysis in America have been constricting influences that have impeded research and fettered inquiry. As Shakow (1965) observed, "A scientific area belongs ultimately to its investigators, not to its practitioners. No field can maintain its vitality, in fact, its viability, without such a group. One of the most cogent criticisms that can be made of psychoanalysis at the present is that it has neglected this indispensable rule for growth" (p. 355). Because of its largely self-imposed isolation, psychoanalysis has deprived itself of the help and collaboration of well-trained investigators and engendered negative attitudes in government and private organizations which control the purse strings of research support. Some of these deficiencies are gradually being remedied (e.g., a somewhat larger number of candidates are receiving analytic training for research purposes), and to some extent thorough training in psychoanalytic therapy and research is available to persons with background training in a variety of fields. Usually this training is conducted by organizations other than the "official" training institutes.

It is quite possible that astounding advances are not to be expected in a field like psychoanalytic therapy. With respect to the problem of personality change, therapists beginning with Freud have been impressed with the generally slow rate of change. Perhaps it bears underscoring that analytic therapy is not aimed at rapid cures but strives for "gradual, unconscious, emotional rearrangements" (Hammett, 1965). Precisely how such rearrangements come about remains unclear, but they do occur and may be broadly viewed as a function of an emotional learning process.

Even in the absence of radically new discoveries, however, systematic inquiries dealing with the selection of patients, the effect of the therapist's attitude, and emotional commitment, the handling of transference manifestations, and the problem of making therapy a maximally meaningful emotional experience are by no means impossible. Many of these problems, despiite great technical and practical difficulties, *are* amenable to research, given the good will, patience, and persistence of investigators working in collaboration with therapists. Advances may come from laboratory investigations and from unsuspected sources. I believe, however, that the predictability of psychotherapeutic outcomes can be significantly enhanced by research conducted *within the framework* of the psychotherapeutic situation. While psychotherapy may be destined to remain a clinical art,[2] it seems reasonable to hope

---

[2] The high level of skill achieved by some practitioners is truly impressive, and better ways should be sought to communicate this expertise.

that its technical tools can be sharpened by investigative efforts. So far, it must be admitted, objective research in the area has had few practical applications for clinical practice. But it must also be kept in mind that psychotherapy is still a young science, with a long historical tradition but a short scientific history.

To indulge in some speculation about promising areas of advance, I would say that the basic discoveries of Freud relating to the dynamic unconscious, the emergence of transference phenomena, and their handling in the unique dyadic relationship of the analytic situation continue to hold our best hope for the future. Among the many unexplored but potentially fruitful approaches I would name:

1. Investigations aimed at studying characteristics of patients for whom this form of therapy is most suitable. Systematic study may serve to restrict psychoanalytic therapy to patients for whom it is clearly applicable and who are most likely to profit from it. Furthermore, systematic investigation along these lines may lead to the development of more specific therapeutic techniques for patients with particular personality structures and problems in living. Such specification is an urgent requirement.

2. Intensive study of variables in the personality of the therapist which, in conjunction with his technique, mediate the therapeutic influence. We may succeed in isolating better methods for ascertaining "patient–therapist compatibility," thus heightening the chances for an emotionally meaningful experience and re-education. Experimentation with variations in technique (coupled with a clearer formulation of technical principles) should be undertaken in the context of the personality of the therapist, from which technique is inseparable.

Advances in these areas are contingent upon the solution of a variety of technical problems, including the measurement of therapeutic change (Luborsky & Schimek, 1964), and specification of the character of the therapeutic influence.

With honest and sustained effort, psychotherapy may show steady progress. Just as any educational process is gradual, so psychotherapeutic changes may remain slow and even tedious. As in the matter of education, not all persons are equally educable. There seems little doubt that for a long time to come problems in living, created or aggravated by untoward interpersonal events in a person's emotional development, can be effectively resolved by more favorable human experiences as provided through psychotherapy. This is not to gainsay the possibility that personality changes can *also* be achieved in other ways, including techniques of psychotherapy based on divergent theoretical assumptions. But analytic psychotherapy, insofar as it remains rooted in empirical observations, aims at a theory of rational and planful personality change which does full justice to the complexities of the human personality. In this respect, it has a great advantage over a variety of simplistic schemes that seem to pre-empt the contemporary scene. What the field can ill afford is an attitude of smugness, an air of finality, or unsupported claims of superiority over all contenders. It may turn out that pharmacological agents or other measures may be more "efficient" for certain purposes than psychotherapy. However, by working toward realistic goals, and by abandoning grandiose aspirations, analytic therapy seems to be assured of its value as a potent weapon in man's continued fight against neurotic suffering and misery. We may be sure that the future will not be utopian, but neither need there be cause for despair.

RESEARCH ON CONTEMPORARY
CLINICAL PRACTICE

In this section I propose to take a closer look at emerging attempts to study at first hand what therapists do in contradistinction to what they say they do. Only during the last quarter of a century have serious efforts been made by researchers in the United States to apply objective methods to the study of therapeutic techniques. I shall primarily draw on research done by our own group to document certain relationships between therapeutic techniques and the therapist personality. In the early stages of psychoanalysis, techniques were treated as separate and distinct from the person applying them. Discussions concerning technique tended to be general and abstract; more recently it has been realized that such statements must be operationally defined, and that statements about the "analysis of transference," "working through," etc. must be more clearly specified than has been done in the past.

Freud's papers on technique, as is well known, were not plentiful, and when he did write on the subject he tended to speak in general terms. Furthermore, there is a reason to believe that Freud's descriptions of technique are not an accurate guide to the manner in which psychoanalysis was practiced by him or anyone else. The descriptions tended to be recommendations rather than statements of what was actually done. It was assumed that *any* analyst, so long as he was properly trained, would follow Freud's technique in essential respects, and that individual difference among therapists were negligi-speak in general terms. Furthermore, there is reason to believe able units, at least as far as their adherence to the basic tenets of psychoanalytic treatment was concerned. To be sure, Freud occasionally mentioned individual differences but assigned to them no great significance except in the context of countertransference reactions. He took it for granted that analyzed therapists were mature, reliable, and responsible individuals who in certain situations could act as mentors or serve as models to their patients. However, in his thinking, the personality of the therapist was tangential and inconsequential to what he perceived to be the essence of psychoanalytic therapy.

The view of therapists as interchangeable units was first challenged in 1938 [3] by Edward Glover (1940) who submitted a lengthy questionnaire to the members of the British Psychoanalytic Association about their therapeutic techniques and practices. The form was sent to 29 practicing analysts, and the survey yielded responses from 24. The results were impressive but should have occasioned no surprise. Briefly, Glover found that British analysts, despite the marked homogeneity of their training, agreed on very few points, and indeed revealed marked divergence on many aspects of technique and practice. Glover has worded his questions in rather general terms and the responses reflected what the British analysts at the time *said* they did—not what they actually did. The *practical* significance of Glover's results is difficult to assess, because although apparent discrepancies may have been of little practical import, the opposite is more likely. In any event, the conclusion was justified that there are true differences in the techniques of therapists of similar training and experience.

There is no reason to assume that the situation is different

---

[3] Anna Freud (1954) reported that "years ago, in Vienna" analysts discovered that they differed widely in their techniques. She states: "So far as I know, no one has succeeded yet in investigating and finding the causes of these particular variations. They are determined, of course, not by the material, but by the trends of interest, intentions, shades of evaluation which are peculiar to every individual analyst. I do not suggest that they should be looked for among the phenomena of countertransference" (p. 609).

today. The limited number of empirical studies bearing on this topic (Strupp, 1955a, 1955b, 1955c) suggest that inexperienced therapists as a group are more "alike" in their techniques than experienced ones following the same theoretical orientation, but that there are differences in technique among therapists following divergent theoretical orientations. One series of studies (Fiedler, 1950a, 1950b, 1951) is often cited in support of the view that experienced therapists, regardless of their theoretical orientation, establish therapeutic relationships whose atmosphere shows greater resemblance than those of novices. However, these findings have at best limited validity. By rigorous criteria, it must be asserted that the question is as yet unanswered.

Primary data on psychotherapeutic techniques, such as transcripts or sound recordings, have been scarce. Prior to 1940 such materials were virtually unavailable, and since that time the situation has not changed substantially, some notable exceptions notwithstanding. Examples of the latter are the sound films of psychoanalytic treatment produced by the late Franz Alexander at Mt. Sinai Hospital in Los Angeles and by Paul Bergman at the National Institute of Mental Health in Bethesda. Comparable records of individual hours or segments of therapy have been somewhat more plentiful, but highly experienced therapists, for the most part, have been rather reluctant to submit their therapeutic operations to public scrutiny. While the privacy of psychotherapy lends justification to the desire to maintain the utmost confidentiality, the fact remains that we are largely uninformed concerning the actual practices of the rank and file of psychotherapists. Thus, it is difficult to form a clear picture of the techniques of the average psychotherapist, nor is it possible to make rigorous comparisons of changes in practices over the years.

An important question concerns the relationship between

a therapist's theoretical assumptions and his technique. To what extent does technique mirror underlying theoretical beliefs and, to what extent is it possible to make inferences about the therapist's theoretical assumptions by studying his behavior with a patient? Ideally, two therapists subscribing to identical theoretical tenets may be expected to employ identical therapeutic techniques. As has been stated, such is not the case. Their communications will diverge on as many dimensions as one is willing to define. These dimensions are frequency of utterances, length, emotional quality, intonation, topics selected for comment—to name but a few. Such dimensions exemplify the kinds of variables which researchers using content analysis have attempted to define and measure over the past twenty years in an effort to compare therapeutic techniques. It may be objected that such measurable differences are not the real ones, since two therapists might differ in their therapeutic styles and yet practice an identical form of therapy. This position is untenable since one may retort, "By what criteria is similarity or difference to be decided?" Surely, it must be more than someone's opinion. Even if one were to rely on such an opinion, the rater or judge will apply, however implicitly, certain criteria which could be precisely the ones needing definition.

The issue is crucial because of the alleged theoretical differences among schools of psychotherapy, which their originators have done their utmost to accentuate. Typically, these systems are also tied to conceptualizations about childhood development and the evolution of the adult personality. Many of these attempts, particularly insofar as they are based on empirical observations, are valuable contributions to the science of psychology, but this is not the present concern. To the extent that these theoretical positions include a theory of psychotherapy that gives rise to specific kinds of therapeutic interventions, these techniques must be operationally definable. Stated otherwise, the assertion that different systems lead to different therapeutic techniques is of little value unless the differences are in some way demonstrable. If a Rogerian, a Sullivanian, and a Freudian practice forms of psychotherapy that do not differ along the particular lines contended by the originators of the system, then the uniqueness of the system may be a myth. To complicate matters, it may also be true that alleged differences in technique may lie along dimensions different from those postulated by the system. In this case the theoretical differences may be of negligible relevance as far as the practice of psychotherapy is concerned, and an entirely different theory of the nature of the psychotherapeutic influence may have to be written. Frank (1961) made a significant attempt to isolate common elements in diverse forms of psychological influence, including psychotherapy, religious conversion, and "brainwashing." Does the problem have to be resolved by recourse to the kinds of *changes* effected by a given form of psychotherapy? Perhaps, but in that event criteria for the measurement of changes have to be evolved. The contention of analysts that orthodox analysis produces a restructuring of the psychic apparatus whereas other forms of therapy achieve modifications that are less far-reaching and profound is plausible, but the critics have a right to be shown that this is indeed the case. Again, it is necessary to develop criteria by which such personality modifications can be reliably and validly judged. Thus far, available methods are woefully inadequate for such an undertaking.

If the nature of the psychological influence exerted by different forms of psychotherapy turns out to have only a loose relationship to the system espoused by the therapist, one may wonder about the nature of the significant dimensions.

One important dimension that invites attention as a strong contender is the person of the therapist, including his attitudes toward the patient. For example, interest, dedication, and investment in the patient as a person and the therapist's ability to make therapy a significant and meaningful experience for the patient are important. *How* he accomplishes this feat is precisely the problem which research in this area must answer. The therapist's depth of belief in the truth and usefulness of his theoretical system and his abiding willingness and faith in his ability to help the patient, as Frank (1961) suggested, probably play an important part. It may also be surmised that, depending on the patient's personality, cultural background and values, different systems of psychotherapy have different degrees of intellectual and ultimately emotional appeal over and beyond the personality of the therapist. This in no way denies the possibility that some conceptions of neurosis and emotional problems in living, apart from the person of the therapist, are more fruitful, heuristic, and capable of effecting deeper personality changes than others.

The critical problem for the researcher is: in order to specify the conditions under which psychotherapy produces specific changes in specific patients, it is necessary to compare different forms of psychotherapy on relevant dimensions. But what are the relevant dimensions?

Since communication between patient and therapist is mediated primarily by linguistic symbols, a first requirement for objective research is to devise conceptual tools that permit the investigator to abstract and quantify relevant aspects of the verbal interchange. Obviously, there are innumerable ways of accomplishing this end, and the measures upon which the investigator decides are as noteworthy for what they leave out as for what they include. The selection is dictated by theoretical as well as practical considerations, and in a sense it represents a prejudgment of what is important to measure. A content-analysis system is therefore not a neutral yardstick and the descriptive measures representing its yield are usually of limited value. Their meaning is enhanced when they are related to other variables, such as measures derived from patient communications, and characteristics of the therapist's personality.

During the past 20 years many content-analysis systems have been developed, which are applicable to patient communications, therapist communications, and both. A comprehensive, critical review of such systems as well as of substantive investigations based on them may be found in Auld and Murray (1955). Dittes (1959) and Marsden (1965) may be consulted for additional references.

Therapist Characteristics

As part of a systematic effort to study the doctor-patient relationship in psychotherapy, nondirective therapists focused upon the therapist's contribution, subjecting his communications during the therapeutic hour to systematic analysis. Snyder (1945) grouped 3600 statements made by nondirective counselors into sixteen categories, which were then grouped into five broader classes representing a directiveness–nondirectiveness continuum. He found that 62.6 per cent of all responses were classifiable as nondirective. Seeman (1949) essentially repeated Snyder's study, using 10 completely recorded cases comprising a total of 60 interviews. He found significant differences in counseling method, the largest shift being in nondirective responses. Seeman's figure was 85 per cent as compared with Synder's 62.6 per cent. Contrary to these findings, Porter (1943) observed quite stable patterns in

the use of counseling techniques from one interview to the
next, and from one counselor to the next, in a given school of
training.

The present writer (Strupp, 1955a) compared Rogerian
and psychoanalytically oriented therapists, using their responses to a series of patient statements presented to them on
cards, and analyzing the data by means of Bales' (1950) system of interaction process analysis. As might be expected,
Rogerians showed a strong predilection for reflection-of-
feeling responses, whereas the second group preferred ex-
ploratory questions. In this sample, experienced Rogerians, as
opposed to inexperienced Rogerians, showed a significant de-
cline in reflection-of-feeling responses, with a concomitant
increase in other response categories. Related comparisons
(Strupp, 1955a, 1955c) showed that the response distributions
of psychologists, social workers, and psychiatrists following
psychoanalytical principles were markedly similar. Experienced therapists tended to give a larger number of interpretations, but their responses were more evenly distributed over a
large number of categories than were those of Rogerians.
Therapists whose training had included a personal analysis
gave fewer silent responses than nonanalyzed therapists gave.
There is reason to believe that the latter finding was a function of the experimental situation, because in a later study
(Strupp, 1958a), which involved therapists' responses to an
entire filmed interview, the findings were reversed.

Strupp (1957b) applied his system of content-analysis
(1957a) to the therapist's interventions in ten actual interviews from a case reported by Wolberg. In a subsequent
paper (Strupp, 1957c), the analysis of the Wolberg interviews
was compared with a similar analysis of a case history reported by Rogers. The quantitative treatment essentially confirmed what would have been predicted from a knowledge

of the theoretical orientations of the two therapists, their expertness, and their characteristic modes of interacting with patients. Nevertheless, the study is apparently a first attempt at comparing the verbal interventions of two therapists of different theoretical orientations.

Strupp (1958b, 1958c) has further documented the differences between therapists in terms of clinical judgments as well as communications attributable to level of experience, professional affiliation (psychologists vs. psychiatrists), theoretical orientation (Rogerians vs. psychoanalytically oriented therapists), and personal analysis.

Fey (1958) studied the responses of 36 therapists representing different theoretical orientations. His questions dealt primarily with common problems of technique. He found the greatest homogeneity among Rogerians (a finding confirmed by Strupp's studies) and the least homogeneity among analysts. Also, greater experience was found to be associated with greater flexibility, which was defined as a disinclination to give extreme responses.

Holt and Luborsky (1958), in their massive effort to predict the overall competence of psychiatric residents, include a statement of the personality characteristics that a good psychiatrist, in the opinion of experts in the field, should possess. They found little specificity to the particular disciplines of psychiatry, psychotherapy, and psychoanalysis; likewise, little differentiation could be made between these characteristics and the qualifications of "the good clinical psychologist" drawn up by a committee of the American Psychological Association. Many statements seemed to characterize the kind of man one might hope to encounter in any profession and who might be expected to do well in almost any type of work. Typical personality attributes were superior intelligence, capacity for understanding, empathy, flexibility, breadth of interests, respect for the dignity and integrity of the individual.

The foregoing sampling of studies suggests that the importance of the therapist variable is being increasingly recognized, although objective research has thus far used relatively gross indices, such as theoretical orientation and level of experience. There is a noteworthy trend, in keeping with the emphasis upon an operational definition of variables, toward taking the actual transactions of the interview situation as the point of departure rather than relying on second-hand reports.

CHARACTERISTICS OF THERAPIST-PATIENT INTERACTION

Every neurotic patient is unconsciously committed to maintaining the status quo. Thus psychotherapy, particularly if aimed at confronting the patient with his inner conflicts, proceeds against powerful unconscious resistances. Unless there is a strong conscious desire to be helped and to collaborate with the therapist, the odds against a favorable outcome may be insuperable. "Motivation for therapy" is a global concept, which may include high intelligence, a relatively intact ego, relative absence of strong secondary gains from one's neurosis, the ability and willingness to withstand frustration and suffering. A certain psychological mindedness, including a readiness to look within oneself for the causes of unhappiness, a strong desire to change coupled with subjective discomfort, freedom from crippling physical diseases, lack of interfering environmental factors, ample financial resources, and youth are also desirable. In addition, such considerations as the nature and extent of the patient's symptomatology and the degree to which it permeates his personality structure enter into prognostic judgments. Because psychotherapy demands great investments of time and emotional energy from the therapist, it is hardly surprising that his willingness to enter into a therapeutic relationship with a particular patient becomes highly selective. Different therapists have highly individual preferences, which it would be important to elucidate. It seems reasonable to assume that therapeutic relationships in which the patient is highly motivated to seek help and in which the therapist is highly motivated to put his skills at the patient's disposal have the greatest chance of success. This is another area in which research may enhance specificity and thereby the effectiveness of psychotherapy.

Kirtner and Cartwright (1958), studying 42 cases treated at the University of Chicago Counseling Center, found a significant association between treatment outcome and the manner in which the client conceptualized and presented his problem in the initial interview. Unsuccessfully treated clients tended to intellectualize; they discussed external manifestations of internal difficulties. Successfully treated clients tended to deal with feelings in the therapeutic relationship and were eager to discover how they themselves were contributing to their inner difficulties. No doubt the second group would be considered more suitable for client-centered therapy. While it cannot be proved, it is entirely possible that those patients who felt they could be helped by client-centered therapists continued to work on their problems, whereas those who did not, dropped out. One may also speculate that the therapist's motivation to help the first group of patients was, for a variety of reasons, weaker. Thus, the therapist's attitude toward the patient may reinforce corresponding attitudes in the patient, which could lead to premature termination of therapy. There is no implication that this phenomenon is restricted to one form of therapy. The judgment of therapeutic failure, premature termination, therapeutic impasse, and poor motivation for therapy wherever they occur may indicate an unwillingness or inability on the part of the therapist to work with a particular patient, as much as it reflects limiting factors within the patient.

Indirect evidence bearing upon this problem was adduced by the author (Strupp, 1958a) in a study of the response of over two hundred therapists to a sound film of an initial interview. Results showed considerable divergence in the respondents' clinical judgments, recommendations for treatment, attitudes toward the patients, and communications addressed to the patient. Systematic differences in therapist responses were traceable to such variables as level of experience and theoretical orientation. However, the therapist's attitude toward the patient, as rated by himself, seemed to be another important source of variance. For example, negative attitudes toward the patient were found to be correlated with a more unfavorable diagnosis and prognosis, with recommendations for greater strictness and activity on the part of the therapist, and with recommendations for less frequent interviews. Significantly, too, therapists who rated their attitude toward the patient as negative tended to show less empathy in their communications. This was particularly true of experienced therapists whose training had not included a personal analysis.

The findings clearly showed that therapists responded differently to the patient, depending on whether his hostile, angry, demanding attitudes stimulated anger and rejection in them. It was possible to differentiate two major groups of therapists, one which appeared more tolerant, more humane, more permissive, more democratic, and perhaps more therapeutic, and a second group which emerged as more directive, more disciplinary, moralistic, and harsh. Those in the first group were warmer in their communications to the patient; concomitantly, cold, rejecting comments were relatively less frequent.

The results also suggested that, to some extent at least, therapists were aware of their positive or negative reactions to the patient and of their willingness or unwillingness to enter into a therapeutic relationship with him. Undoubtedly they were less aware of the manner in which their attitude interacted with their clinical evaluations. In the light of this evidence, one begins to speculate about the extent to which the therapist's attitude, as conveyed by his communications to the patient, tends to bring about a realization of the therapist's expectations in actual therapy situations. For psychotherapy, the crux of the matter is not the perceptions and clinical evaluations, nor even the therapist's conscious attitude toward the patient; rather, it is the manner in which these variables influence and structure the therapeutic relationship. This, clearly, is an important problem requiring much further exploration.

Patient Characteristics

A number of studies (Rubinstein and Lorr, 1956; Frank et al., 1957; Imber et al., 1956; Lorr, Katz, and Rubinstein, 1958) have presented converging evidence on those characteristics of patients that, actuarially, make them good candidates for psychotherapy. These people tend to be well educated, articulate, and socially responsible; they are members of the middle class, have a considerable degree of ego strength, are not deriving excessive secondary gains from their neurotic difficulties via incapacitating somatic illnesses, are anxious, and are eager to do something about their problems. This does not mean, except in a superficial sense, that they are "well" or "normal." These people are chronically disturbed in their interpersonal relations and extremely unhappy in their personal and professional lives. The trouble is that society and "objective" science have no adequate yardsticks for measuring personal unhappiness, nor do they usually pay much attention to it. Parenthetically, one of the flagrant shortcomings of the traditional "outcome" studies in psychotherapy is that they largely ignore the patient's subjective feelings of improvement. This is partly the patient's fault, if one may use this term, because frequently he is hard put, after significant therapeutic improvement, to recall his former state of distress.

The available evidence substantiates Freud's original dictum about the limited applicability of intensive forms of psychotherapy. Psychoanalysis, as the most ambitious and far-reaching attempt at restructuring the personality, makes the most stringent demands upon the qualifications of both the patient and the therapist. But other forms of psychotherapy, insofar as they are aimed at emotional insight, also presuppose a fairly intact ego in the patient, and most of the characteristics already mentioned. From everything that has been said, it is apparent that psychotherapy, even with considerable modification, is applicable only to a relatively limited segment of the total population. It has been pointed out that most theories and principles of psychotherapy embody middle-class objectives and values. Hollingshead and Redlich's (1958) investigations corroborate these assertions from a different vantage point. They demonstrate, among other things, that the form of therapy a patient receives tends to be correlated with social class membership. Thus, psychotherapy is the therapy of choice for members of the upper middle class, whereas the somatic therapies, particularly in the case of psychotic patients, are more characteristic of the person belonging to lower social classes. It must be remembered, however, that social class is merely one of the variables that enter into judgments of a patient's suitability for psychotherapy. There can be little doubt that prospective patients are more likely to be accepted for psychotherapy if they meet most of the criteria characterizing the good psychotherapy patient. In addition, psychiatrists and psychologists subscribe to an implicit ranking of neurotic and characterological conditions according to their alleged treatability. Without attempting a thorough discussion of this complex problem, it may be stated that, beginning with Freud, the classical neurotic conditions, like hysteria, are considered ideally suitable for psychotherapy and psychoanalysis. However, severe character disorders and the psychoses are generally considered unsuitable. Such subjective classifications reflect clinical experience. They may reflect value judgments about the kind of persons psychotherapists "prefer" to work with, as well as an appraisal in sociocultural terms of the conditions they are suffering from. Consequently, a patient meeting the psychotherapist's explicit as well as implicit criteria of good or promising not only has a better chance of finding a competent therapist, but he may from the beginning elicit greater interest from the therapist, which may be reflected in greater willingness to make an emotional investment in the patient and to devote greater energy to the treatment.

It is as yet unknown to what extent the patient may fulfill the therapist's unverbalized prophecy. It is, however, clear that without a keen and abiding interest and dedication on the part of the therapist, the patient cannot marshal the necessary strength and energy to fight his way to a healthier adaptation. This is particularly true in those situations in which the therapist aims at a thorough reorganization of the patient's personality through the reliving of his childhood traumas. Too, the infinite patience that dedicated therapists like Frieda Fromm-Reichmann, Otto Will, Harold Searles, and others have invested in therapy with schizophrenic patients bears eloquent tribute to the proposition that therapeutic gains are often commensurate with the efforts expended by the therapist, provided the patient possesses basic personality resources.

On a smaller scale, numerous studies attest that patients who appear to be motivated for psychotherapy tend to be better liked by therapists and the prognosis is seen as more favorable (Wallach and Strupp, 1960). Heine and Trosman (1960) have shown that mutuality of expectation is an important factor in the continuation of the therapeutic relationship. In this study, patients who continued in psychotherapy conceptualized their expectations of therapy in a manner more congruent with the therapist's role image, and may therefore have been more gratifying to the therapist. Similarly, Strupp and Williams (1960) found that patients who were judged nondefensive, insightful, likable, and well motivated for therapy were seen by therapists as most likely to improve. In the same vein, Sullivan, Miller, and Smelser (1958) summed up their findings by saying: "Those persons who are least equipped to meet life challenges are the ones who stand to gain least from psychotherapy."

Conclusions as to Research in Clinical Practice

In the foregoing I have presented some examples of the steadily increasing research effort in psychotherapeutic practice. Clearly, research in psychotherapy is at an early stage of development. It is groping, and it suffers from many conceptual and methodological deficiencies. At the same time, it continues to offer a momentous challenge to the clinically oriented experimental psychologist. However, as Rapaport (1960) points out in a perceptive discussion, sophistication and advances in knowledge cannot be achieved by means of ad hoc quantifications based upon an inadequate understanding of complex processes, no matter how sophisticated one's methodology may be:

If logic, methodology, and mathematics were the pacemakers of development in sciences, this development could be fast enough in psychology. But the pacemaker is not methodology—it is human invention. . . . Methodology, since it deals with relationships of concepts, all of which are potentially valid, can go on continuously, building ever-new castles in Spain. But human invention consists of discontinuous events, each of which requires long preparation, since in it an individual's thought patterns must come to grips with patterns of nature, and only those rare encounters in which a unique human thought pattern actually matches a unique pattern of nature will matter. If the match is not specific and precise, or if the individual is not prepared to recognize it, or if he does recognize it but is not ready to use it, the moment is lost" (pp. 37-38).

Mindful of Rapaport's injunction, research in this area should beware of pseudo-quantifications, which often tend to close prematurely an area of inquiry and give rise to the illusion that a problem has been solved when the exploration has barely begun. In studying doctor-patient relationships in psychotherapy, there is much room for patient, naturalistic observation and for a careful mapping out of variables. Morison's (1960) wise counsel to the scientist for "gradualness, gradualness, gradualness" is likewise germane. Above all, it seems to this writer, the researcher should strive for a greater awareness of the proposition that research concerned with doctor-patient relationships and psychotherapy deals specifically and uniquely with human problems—with the complexities of human psychology and with the problems of human adaptation to other human beings. If this be true, there can be no simple substitutes or translations from laboratory research, animal studies, or conditioning experiments, much as these may advance psychological science in other respects.

REFERENCES

Auld, F., Jr., and Murray, E. J. Content-analysis studies of psychotherapy. *Psychological Bulletin,* 1955, 52, 377–395.

Bales, R. F. *Interaction process analysis.* Reading, Mass.: Addison-Wesley, 1950.

Breger, L., and McGaugh, J. L. Critique and reformulation of "learning-theory" approaches to psychotherapy and neurosis. *Psychological Bulletin,* 1965, 63, 338–358.

Dittes, J. E. Previous studies bearing on content analysis of psychotherapy. In J. Dollard & F. Auld, Jr., *Scoring human motives.* New Haven: Yale University Press, 1959. Pp. 325–351.

Eissler, K. R. *Medical orthodoxy and the future of psychoanalysis.* New York: International Universities Press, 1965.

Eysenck, H. J. The effects of psychotherapy: An evaluation. *Journal of Consulting Psychology,* 1952, 16, 319–324.

Eysenck, H. J. Learning theory and behavior therapy. *Journal of Mental Science,* 1959, 105, 61–75.

Eysenck, H. J. The effects of psychotherapy. In H. J. Eysenck (Ed.), *Handbook of abnormal psychology.* New York: Basic Books, 1961, pp. 697–725.

Fey, W. F. Doctrine and experience: Their influence upon the psychotherapist. *Journal of Consulting Psychology,* 1958, 22, 403–409.

Fiedler, F. The concept of an ideal therapeutic relationship. *Journal of Consulting Psychology,* 1950a, 14, 239–245.

Fiedler, F. A comparison of therapeutic relationships in psychoanalytic, nondirective, and Adlerian therapy. *Journal of Consulting Psychology*, 1950b, 14, 436–445.

Fiedler, F. Factor analyses of psychoanalytic, nondirective and Adlerian therapeutic relationships. *Journal of Consulting Psychology*, 1951, 15, 32–38.

Ford, D. H., and Urban, H. B. *Systems of psychotherapy: A comparative study.* New York: John Wiley & Sons, 1963.

Frank, J. D. *Persuasion and healing: A comparative study of psychotherapy.* Baltimore: Johns Hopkins Press, 1961.

Frank, J. D., Gliedman, L. H., Imber, S. D., Nash, E. H., Jr., and Stone, A. R. Why patients leave psychotherapy. *Archives of Neurology and Psychiatry*, 1957, 77, 283–299.

Freud, Anna. The widening scope of indications for psychoanalysis: Discussion. *Journal of American Psychoanalytic Association*, 1954, 2, 607–620.

Glover, E. (1940). Common technical practices: A questionnaire research. In E. Glover, *The technique of psycho-analysis.* New York: International Universities Press, 1955, pp. 261–350.

Hammett, V. O. A consideration of psychoanalysis in relation to psychiatry generally, circa 1965. *American Journal of Psychiatry*, 1965, 122, 42–54.

Harper, R. A. *Psychoanalysis and psychotherapy: 36 systems.* Englewood Cliffs, N. J.: Prentice-Hall, 1959.

Heine, R. W., and Trosman, H. Initial expectations of the doctor-patient interaction as a factor in continuance in psychotherapy. *Psychiatry*, 1960, 23, 275–278.

Hollingshead, A. B., and Redlich, F. C. *Social class and mental illness.* New York: Wiley, 1958.

Holt, R. R., and Luborsky, L. *Personality patterns of psychiatrists.* New York: Basic Books, 1958.

Imber, S. D., Frank, J., Gliedman, L., Nash, E., and Stone, A. Suggestibility, social class, and acceptance of psychotherapy. *Journal of Clinical Psychology*, 1956, 12, 341–344.

Kirtner, W. L., and Cartwright, D. S. Success and failure in client-centered therapy as a function of initial in-therapy behavior. *Journal of Consulting Psychology*, 1958, 22, 329–333.

Krasner, L., and Ullman, L. P. (Eds.). *Research in behavior modification: New developments and implications.* New York: Holt, Rinehart & Winston, 1965.

Lorr, M., Katz, M. N., and Rubinstein, E. A. The prediction of length of stay in psychotherapy. *Journal of Consulting Psychology*, 1958, 22, 321–327.

Luborsky, L., and Schimek, Jean. Psychoanalytic theories of therapeutic and developmental change: Implications for assessment. In P. Worchel and D. Byrne, (Eds.), *Personality change.* New York: John Wiley, 1964. Pp. 73–99.

Marmor, J. Psychoanalytic therapy as an educational process. In J. H. Masserman (Ed.), *Psychoanalytic education.* New York: Grune & Stratton, 1962.

Marsden, G. Content-analysis studies of therapeutic interviews. 1954 to 1964. *Psychological Bulletin*, 1965, 63, 298–321.

May, R., Angel, E., and Ellenberger, H. F. *Existence: A new dimension in psychiatry and psychology.* New York: Basic Books, 1958, pp. 37–91.

Morison, R. S. "Gradualness, gradualness, gradualness" (I. P. Pavlov). *American Psychologist*, 1960, 15, 187–197.

Porter, E. H., Jr. The development and evaluation of a measure of counseling and interview procedures. *Educational and Psychological Measurement*, 1943, 3, 105–125; 215–238.

Rapaport, D. The structure of psychoanalytic theory: A systematizing attempt. *Psychological Issues*, 1960, 2, No. 2.

Rubinstein, E., and Lorr, M. A comparison of terminators and remainers in outpatient psychotherapy. *Journal of Clinical Psychology*, 1956, 12, 345–349.

Seeman, J. A. A study of the process of nondirective therapy. *Journal of Consulting Psychology*, 1949, 13, 157–168.

Shakow, D. Seventeen years later: Clinical psychology in the light of the 1947 Committee on Training in Clinical Psychology Report. *American Psychologist*, 1965, 20, 353–362.

Snyder, W. U. An investigation of the nature of non-directive psychotherapy. *Journal of Genetic Psychology*, 1945, 33, 193–223.

Strupp, H. H. An objective comparison of Rogerian and psychoanalytic techniques. *Journal of Consulting Psychology*, 1955a, 19, 1–7.

Strupp, H. H. Psychotherapeutic technique, professional affiliation, and experience level. *Journal of Consulting Psychology*, 1955b, 19, 197–202.

Strupp, H. H. The effect of the psychotherapist's personal analysis upon his techniques. *Journal of Consulting Psychology*, 1955c, 19, 197–204.

Strupp, H. H. A multidimensional system for analyzing psychotherapeutic techniques. *Psychiatry*, 1957a, 20, 293–306.

Strupp, H. H. A multidimensional analysis of techniques in brief psychotherapy. *Psychiatry*, 1957b, 20, 387–397.

Strupp, H. H. A multidimensional comparison of therapist activity in analytic and client-centered therapy. *Journal of Consulting Psychology*, 1957c, 21, 301–308.

Strupp, H. H. The psychotherapist's contribution to the treatment process. *Behavioral Science*, 1958a, 3, 34–67.

Strupp, H. H. The performance of psychoanalytic and client-centered therapists in an initial interview. *Journal of Consulting Psychology*, 1958b, 22, 265–274.

Strupp, H. H. The performance of psychiatrists and psychologists in a therapeutic interview. *Journal of Clinical Psychology*, 1958c, 14, 219–226.

Strupp, H. H., and Williams, Joan V. Some determinants of clinical evaluations of different psychiatrists. *Archives of General Psychiatry*, 1960, 2, 434–440.

Sullivan, P. L., Miller, Christine, and Smelser, W. Factors in
length of stay and progress in psychotherapy. *Journal of
Consulting Psychology*, 1958, 22, 1–9.

Szasz, T. S. *The myth of mental illness: Foundations of a theory
of personal conduct.* New York: Paul B. Hoeber, 1961.

Ullman, L. P., and Krasner, L. (Eds.). *Case studies in behavior
modification.* New York: Holt, Rinehart & Winston, 1965.

Wallach, M. S., and Strupp, H. H. Psychotherapists' clinical judgments and attitudes towards patients. *Journal of Consulting
Psychology*, 1960, 24, 316–323.

Watson, R. I. The experimental tradition and clinical psychology.
In A. J. Bachrach (Ed.), *Experimental foundations of clinical
psychology.* New York: Basic Books, 1962. Pp. 3–25.

Wolpe, J. *Psychotherapy by reciprocal inhibition.* Stanford,
Calif.: Stanford University Press, 1958.

3

CURRENT CONTROVERSIES IN PSYCHOANALYTIC GROUP PSYCHOTHERAPY AND WHAT THEY MASK

MAX ROSENBAUM

SINCE WORLD WAR II the field of group psychotherapy has grown tremendously, as has the literature on group psychotherapy. In 1953 one careful researcher was able to unearth 1200 papers in group psychotherapy.[1] By the end of 1955 the group psychotherapy literature consisted of 1700 references. The present annual rate is about 200 books, articles, and theses—double the rate of 1950. Rosenbaum and Hartley (1959, 1962) researched the practices of group psycho-

---

[1] Personal communication from R. J. Corsini

therapists and found many influences at work in their practice. A good deal of confusion was also evident.

Important major points of view in the field of group
psychotherapy have influenced many current workers. For
example, Moreno values enthusiasm, activity, interaction, role-
playing, and spontaneity. Slavson's disciplined approach emphasizes the careful selection of patients, adherence to strict
methodology, curative processes, and carefully determined
goals. To a mixed group of adult patients, Wolf applies
orthodox psychoanalytic conceptions, techniques, and aims.
These three approaches are to be found in much of current
group psychotherapy.

Until recently little attention has been given to the philosophical position that the therapist takes on group treatment.
Current controversy revolves around the immediate experiencing in the group setting and its value for patients as well
as for the group therapist. The question of the total involvement of the therapist has been the interest of such workers as
Mullan (1955), Rosenbaum (1952), and Whitaker and Malone (1953). The direction of this concern is toward a
humanism in psychotherapy. Van Dusen (1957) has given a
detailed picture of existential analysis and its impact upon
European psychiatry. Hora (1959) describes existential
group psychotherapy as a living, dynamic experience in
which the group represents a microcosm of the world; the
loneliness and isolation that patients experience are part of
the total anxiety the world experiences. Hill (1958) has
stressed the importance of the human experience as part of
group psychotherapy. Lyons (1961) reviewed the claims
made for existential pychotherapy and attempted an assessment of its present status and future prospects. He concluded
that "existential psychotherapy today is more gaudy fiction
than fact; yet it remains a hope." Unfortunately, Lyons

started with, but never really accepted, the fact that existential psychotherapy is not one system or school and cannot
be criticized as such. Nelson (1961) in a very extensive summary of existential psychotherapy criticized it bitterly. Friedman in a paper on existential psychotherapy and the image
of man (1965) points out that existentialism is not a philosophy but

a mood embracing a number of disparate philosophies, the
difference between which are more basic than the temper which
unites them. This temper can best be described as a reaction
against the static, the abstract, the purely rational, the merely
irrational, in favor of the dynamic and the concrete, personal
involvement and engagement, action, choice and commitment
and the actual situation of the existential subject as the starting
point of thought.

Kierkegaard, Heidegger, and Sartre emphasize the sub-
jectivity while Martin Buber, Marcel, and Jaspers emphasize
dialogue or communication. What probably binds existential
psychotherapists together is their common enemy, orthodox
psychoanalysis. The existentialists have questioned the meanings of such terms as transference, cure, and healing. Buber
(1957) makes the important point:

An individual is just a certain uniqueness of a human being. . . .
He may become more and more an individual without making
him more and more human. . . . But a person, I would say, is an
individual living really with the world. And with the world I
don't mean in the world, but just in real contact, in real rec-
iprocity. . . . (p. 96).

The major differences and controversies in the field of
psychoanalytic group psychotherapy are apparently between
those who practice a therapy that stresses the patient's in-
tellect and those that emphasize the patient's feelings. The

therapy that emphasizes feelings is called experiential. The two opposing points of view may be found in those who emphasize the intellectual and those who emphasize the affective. It is interesting that psychoanalysts who adopt an experiential approach to group psychotherapy have much the same feeling for the therapeutic process that Carl Rogers (1957) has expressed. It is expressly stated in the experiential approach that the therapist has a value system and he must be aware that directly or indirectly his value system is expressed in the course of group therapy. The experiential approach stresses the reparative forces at work *within* the patient. Thus, Warkentin (1956) introduces the therapist's aggression into psychotherapy with neurotics and psychotics. He stresses confrontation with no relief given to immediate distress. He points out that nonreassuring behavior is contrary to the popular belief that establishment of a useful transference relationship early in therapy with neurotics requires accepting and nonthreatening attitudes on the part of the therapist. He cautions that this technique must be used only by experienced therapists and with neurotics and not psychotics. Really, Warkentin is discussing authenticity with patients. Others who have covered this area from a more traditional analytic view are Winnicot (1949) and Wexler (1951). Contrast this with the short-term conditioned reflex therapy of Wolpe (1958) and his students (Lazarus, 1961), who emphasize the importance of treating specific symptoms. It would seem that the advocates of conditioned reflex therapy emphasize a static approach. They forget that monkeys may make good jockeys but cannot invent the rules of horse racing. Also, those existentialists who reduce problems to completely individualized meanings seem to forget the force of culture.

The current reaction to experiential psychotherapy

may be found in the effort to link contemporary psycho-therapy with logical positivism. Freud lived and worked at the outset of his enterprise in a climate where Darwin had left a great impact. Science was the great word and to be scientific was to be positive. Since Freud was a neurologist, he hunted for facts, positive and unassailable. Just before his death, Freud wrote and showed awareness that his strict biological, instinctual approach could not encompass all the problems of human relatedness. He seemed to have made a great effort to stay away from metaphysical and mystical thought. His every effort was to make the therapist objective. His fear was that the subjective therapist would be involved in counter-transference and counter-transference was per-ceived, like transference, to be rigid, compulsive, archaic, and obstructive of therapy. But this overpreoccupation with the rational often denies man's feeling for man. Einstein is quoted as having said, "The most beautiful emotion we can experience is the mystical. It is the power of all true art and science" (Frank, 1947).

Today we may say that contemporary psychotherapy, whether analytic or not, is engaged in a struggle between the Locke tradition in psychology, with its emphasis on the mind as a mere recipient of stimuli, and the Leibnitz tradition, which conceives of the human mind as self-propelling. The idea that a drug may be primarily beneficial because of the influence of the giver rather than the drug itself (Frank, 1961) is very threatening to those who look for exact answers. Two analysts became so concerned at what they viewed as the menace of "irrational psychotherapy," as they called experiential psychotherapy, that they gave four lectures and published a lengthy series of articles attacking the "menace" (Wolf and Schwartz, 1958). A group of ex-periential psychotherapists (Malone, Whitaker, Warkentin and Felder, 1961) answered this attack by pointing out that the practice of psychiatry is not necessarily the practice of psychotherapy. A psychotherapy which is depth oriented moves toward the reconstructive and toward basic change in the individual who comes as a patient. There is a basic optimism concerning the growth potential of the patient and considerable skepticism toward a more orthodox, Freudian, instinct-based concept of human behavior.

Recently, an orthodox Freudian analyst described to the writer why patients come for therapy. He stated that the patient "is not potent." I commented, "The patient *feels* that he is not potent. His hope is often minimal." The analyst again said, "He *is* not potent." The orthodox analyst's comment embodies his perception of the patient. When asked why patients would be encouraged to return for therapy after they have completed analysis, the orthodox analyst replied, "Because I know more and am more expert. I am a physician and I read and study." There you have it. This intelligent and sensitive man, who also practices group therapy, believes that he continues to be the doctor, and he does not accept that therapy finally moves to a peer relationship. He believes that when the chips are down his knowledge makes him more expert. This internationally known and very experienced analyst confuses an essential point—to be an expert about living does not mean that one is expert in living. If we believe that growth is inexorable in every person, we must finally believe in a process of mutualism in therapy. This means that two living persons are present with one another in a therapy relationship. There can only be feeling that keeps these two people together. The therapist can only be reimbursed for his time but never for his interest and concern. He is spending his life with the patient, who is a person.

The confusion that exists in some quarters concerning the intent of psychotherapy is dissipated by a consideration of treatment goals. The kind of therapeutic aim sought and expected not only serves to clarify the procedure that is to be used but also indicates the expected depth or intensity of the therapy as well as its final outcome. The aim of therapy must always be considered when the efficacy of treatment is being determined.

The regressive-constructive approach centers upon the possibility that the patient will become responsible not only for himself but also for society. The emphasis in the experiential affective approach is on the patient's responsibility as a creator of his culture and as a transmitter of patterns of behavior. To achieve this, his personality must continue to change in an evolving way after formal therapy has ended.

The therapy which emphasizes repression and construction also encourages the patient to develop some responsibility for himself, but at the same time there is an acceptance of rational authority, which is for the "good of all." Adaptation and adjustment play a more striking role than in the intensive affective regressive-reconstructive therapies. The patient's major task in life for the more intellective therapy is considered to be the transmission of culture but not necessarily the creation of a new element in culture. Patients leave therapy at different levels of growth, at the level of intellectual awareness, at the level of emotional insight, and at the level where values are quite spontaneously reassessed and re-evaluated. While these goals are more circumscribed than in the regressive, experiential therapies, they nonetheless are important, valid, and rewarding to the patient. To be relieved of symptoms, to develop a respect for rational authority, to be adapted and adjusted to one's potential and environment, are goals worthy of both patient and therapist. The experiential therapists appear to want larger goals.

Finally, whether rational and intellective or affective and experiential, group psychotherapy, in its similarity to a small society and family, emphasizes both cultural and social responsibility, reminding the members at all times that their *activity* and *creativity* occur through the development of a new behavior for themselves, but *in concert with others*. I want to make it clear that to be in concert with others is not to deny creativity. The oneness of the individual is not to be denied. Concert is not a repressive force as I see it. The creative individual must often be a pioneer. However, it is hoped that while the creative individual creates first for himself, his work finally reaches a culture which may or may not understand him or his productivity. Ideally, he should be able to cope with that culture.

What these controversies finally bring to the forefront is apparently the problem of values. From the early "mirror image" concept of Freud, there has been a movement in contemporary psychotherapy toward evaluating the therapist's personality and his impact upon the patient-person. While this movement is commendable, it seems to miss the boat. The larger issue concerns the entire philosophy of living. Rogers (1961) sensed this struggle when he stated that the kind of world which many behavioral scientists expect and hope for would destroy the kind of person that he has come to know in the deepest moments of psychotherapy—a person who is spontaneous, aware of his freedom to choose who he will be, and aware also of the consequences of his choice. Thus Rogers is disturbed about goals where the limited objectives are productivity, happiness, and submissiveness, which must lead to the "closed society" Orwell has described in

"*1984*," or B. F. Skinner described in *Walden Two*. Rogers stresses as his goal "man as a process of becoming and self-actualization." But this is another sort of "closed society." It is a short step from the logical positivism of early Freudian thinking to the equally specific humanism of Rogers or Fromm (1956). For example, although Fromm is aware that many patients come to psychoanalysis expecting to find magic help and the illusory button that lights up the world, he continues to offer the button. Fromm (1956) states, "There is no meaning to life except the meaning man himself gives to it" (p. 72). This begins to establish a humanistic religion centered around man and his strength. Psychotherapy deludes both practitioner and patient when it offers this answer. All that it can finally do is to emphasize the uniqueness of man so that he may move forward to face the paradoxes, absurdity, and often the despair of life.

Is progress made when we replace an objectivism, with its illusions of hope, for a humanism, with its promises of self-actualization? All that an intensive regressive psychotherapy may reasonably offer to the patient is the opportunity to explore his uniqueness and to use this uniqueness to commit himself to the present and the struggle with the present. Each patient must finally discover, like Job with religion, that intensive psychotherapy offers only the opportunity to face the despair, absurdity, action, and it is hoped, the pleasure in life.

The confusion among different approaches to psychotherapy becomes more and more obvious. Thus, Schwartz (1964) concludes:

After many years of clinical practice and the observation of my own patients and those of my students, I have become convinced that the kind of therapy we do is intimately connected with the kind of person we are, our value systems, our philosophy of life. Each of us has some small personal vision which seems to influ-

ence the way we function as persons and professional practitioners.

In a recent article, Shattan et al. (1966) state,

The supportive nature of the group was fostered by the therapists who tended to be warm, active and giving, rather than silent, neutral and analytic. The therapists served as identification
models and were responsive as "people" rather than as "therapists." The therapists tried to establish an aura of hopefulness and
good feeling rather than to concentrate on the illness of the various group members. We did not ignore illness, however. When
illness appeared, we helped patients to deal with it in a more
realistic manner (p. 803).

How the philosophical system of the therapist invades
psychotherapy becomes critical as we move further. Michael
Reagan has written an article in the *New York Times Magazine* (1966) on the theme that "Washington Should Pay
Taxes to the Poor." The article is devoted to a discussion of
the negative income tax, a new idea in social welfare legisla-
tion to speed up the war on poverty. In the body of the article Reagan writes:

Objections are likely to range from the moral to the material.
The Protestant ethic traditionally (but perhaps diminishingly)
follows the philosophy of no work, no income. Yet we have
really abandoned that principle, through unemployment and dis-
ability compensation, as well as public assistance.

This opinion of Reagan's has far-reaching implications.
Especially when we consider the concepts of learning theory,
reward and punishment, and their relationship to psychotherapy. The example I have cited is very pertinent to the
issue of personal growth and change. The economy of the
United States is based on free enterprise. What is the motivation for people to work if they will be paid without work-

ing? Does the motivation go back to creativity? Of course, this becomes difficult in a culture which increasingly divorces the means from the ends. Perhaps there is a note of anger in the behavior of people who refuse to work. Since many workers are deprived of the opportunity to be part of the end product and are merely part of an assembly line, perhaps the only way they can express anger to a culture which relegates them to machine status is to insist on increasing their dependency. The question intrigues me as to the why of such behavior in a democracy. Examine the contrast in a culture where the people ostensibly live under a dictatorship. In the same issue of the *New York Times*, Tad Szulc describes the search for a missing atomic bomb, lost off the coast of Spain. Szulc points out that the government of the United States will indemnify the villagers of Palomares for losses sustained. He writes, "But while the villagers are aware of the Americans' good wishes, as Mayor Jose Manuel Gonzales Fernandez said the other day, 'We want to work in our fields and earn our own livelihood and not collect payments and be idle.'"

This is an interesting sidelight on the Spanish Catholic culture as contrasted with the American Protestant (Weber, 1965) ethic and its "new" modifications. Therefore, psychotherapy in the United States avoids rather consistently the issues involved in the treatment of people who are emotionally distressed. Psychotherapists themselves appear to avoid the issues which relate to their own value systems. The search for the illusory answers of logical positivism has proven fruitless. Shallow humanism is equally dishonest. Just what does a term like "unconditional positive regard" (Rogers, 1957) mean? Psychotherapists increasingly acknowledge that they have value systems, and a few explore what this means for the theory and practice of psychotherapy. Those who have not thought through the problem of what motivates them in life are ready, or should be ready, to explore this.

It is my impression that there is a tremendous moral dissolution in modern society. The existentialist ethic of Heidegger, Jaspers, Sartre, and Buber contains an individualistic bias. It is clearly stated that the individual, in order to fulfill his potentialities, must come to grips and liberate himself from the weights of an impersonal society. The nucleus of the existential analysis of contemporary man is freedom that entails responsibility. Man cannot be liberated from the mechanical, impersonal world with its artificial objectivity without authentic social participation. Buber stressed this in his phrase, "All real living is meeting."

How is a patient to experience authenticity with a therapist who is confused about his authenticity and has learned technical terms and concepts to mask his confusion and panic? For example, how many therapists have thought through the meaning of opposition to suicide? If there is a commitment to life, what is the life? A physician takes the Hippocratic oath and pledges to maintain life. But what life? Is he saving a biological organism only? And what are psychotherapists saving? Facts do no generate moral judgments. Clinical techniques demonstrate the *how* and not the *whether*.

Recently I was asked to serve as a discussant for a study on the use of untrained and trained psychotherapists in the treatment of schizophrenics in a mental hospital. It would be irrelevant to explore the limitations of the study. What is relevant to me is the confusion concerning the term "psychotherapy." Since we are concerned with the theory and practice of psychotherapy, it is important to note how often, in the study I have mentioned, compassion and humaneness are considered psychotherapy. It has always seemed to me that these qualities are part of maturity and not part of any special aspect of psychotherapy. The psychotherapy that I am thinking of is the psychotherapy that moves the individual to change, and change means a new way of living.

It seems to me that there is a lot of gibberish in psychotherapy which masks the question of why are we here, what are we feeling at this moment in time and space. Perhaps the advent of the nuclear bomb has led some biologists and physicists to become more concerned about what they are doing. Bentley Glass (1965), the investigator of human genetics, has stated, among other things, ". . . ethical values do grow out of the biological nature of man and his evolution." It may sound unreal to some of my readers, but there is an atomic-bomb quality to the intimacy of psychotherapy, and the ethical issues are no less stupendous.

Recently I had the occasion to review a book, *Psychoanalytic Pioneers*. (Alexander et al., 1966). The most striking thing about the descriptions of the early workers in psychoanalysis is the ethic they brought to the field. They did not attempt to find an ethic in the field as so many, if not the majority, of contemporary psychotherapists do. The concern with the neurotic qualities in the religious experience, as, for example, Theodor Reik's studies (1958a, 1958b), should not blind any of us to a recognition of the search for an ethic. Let me make it clear that I am not suggesting, as I feel some of my more naive colleagues advise, "Let us pray" or "Think positively" or "Think sensibly." The almost religious search for logical positivism may lead us to an equally fruitless search in overstructured religion. And by overstructured, I refer to religion that leaves no room for personal searching, but becomes a "Sunday ethic." There is no internalization of the meaning of the religion for "Sunday ethic" parishioners. Permit me to distinguish again between looking for an ethic in psychotherapy and turning to psychotherapy as a way of developing an ethic. Let me point out here that I am writing of ethics and not values. Many psychotherapists confuse the two terms. Values are culturally determined. Ethics deals with two questions: What kinds of things are morally right and good, and what is the nature of moral rightness and goodness.

To illustrate the confusion in training, let me note the following vignette. A psychiatrist listening to a first draft of this paper was upset because I had not listed in the references the current interest in value systems. I became aware that he did not understand the difference between ethic and value. The value is culturally determined and cannot create an ethic. Of course, the ethic is basic and leads to the value. This common confusion among behavioral scientists with whom I have worked indicates a deepseated confusion. For example, the man who experiments with LSD and kills his mother-in-law cannot avoid the question of responsibility when he decided to take the LSD. He may not be punished for acting under the influence of LSD, but is he to be punished for the decision he made in using the LSD? The more I read about what psychotherapists profess to know, the more frightened I become. Are they attempting to create a new religion? Perhaps something is being avoided. Originally, psychology came from philosophy and biology, and perhaps the return after the dalliance with biology is to the philosophical roots. Freud was always concerned about psychoanalysis becoming the handmaiden of psychiatry, submerged in medicine. Perhaps in his own search for clarity about his ethic, and he did have an ethic, he sensed the larger danger involved when psychotherapy itself becomes an ethic. Freud was moved by and always maintained a deep feeling for Oskar Pfister, the Swiss minister and educator who combined psychoanalysis with what he perceived to be his Christian eros, love for one's neighbor. Interestingly enough, Adler, who broke with Freud so violently, acknowledged throughout the years that his individual psychology was changing to a "psychology of values." It is important to note that Ernest Jones, the devoted follower of Freud, always had a deep interest in the psychological foundations of ethics (1910).

Jones (1948) noted that as illusions born of ignorance are dispelled, humility before the unknown increases. Jones' personal atheism appears to me to have been his own unresolved relationship to his father and mother. He did distinguish between superstition and religion, which he felt was one of the means where man copes with guilt and fear. Jones (1951) remarked on "the flood of curves and statistics that threatens to suffocate the science of psychology." Thus he pointed to those psychologists who display a "striking ignorance of the human mind" and, because they lack creative powers, often tend to make up for their deficiencies by inventing "objective methods . . . that are to make them independent of intuition" (pp. 254–255).

It has been noted that Ernest Jones daydreamed in his later years that in the future the analyst or medical psychologist, like the priest of ancient times, might serve as a source of practical wisdom and a stabilizing influence in this chaotic world. Apparently, according to Jones, the community would consult this figure before embarking on any important social or political enterprise. It would seem that the devout atheist Ernest Jones was not above founding his own religion.

So here we have psychotherapists embarking on the deepest voyages into the darkness of man's psyche and soul without the humility I would believe to be appropriate. Witness if you will the proliferation of new therapies, from rational-emotive to conditioned reflex. Is this a search for treatment or a search for an ethic? For a long time in the field of psychotherapy I experienced a kind of irritation and cynicism. Cult after cult seemed to be springing up. Almost like the troubles of the tribes of ancient Israel, all kinds of strange religions were competing. No sooner was one therapy approach found as the panacea, than another new miracle would appear, described as a "newer" therapy approach. I wondered, was it all truly the scientific quest? Was it something more than just a new antibiotic to replace the last miraculous one that didn't turn out to be so miraculous? Are all these new ways of entering Valhalla?

Are new heavens constantly being created by competitive therapists who are excluded from the overcrowded last one? Is it all a game? Or is there a frantic, almost desperate need to find an ethic for psychotherapy? Are therapists duplicating in their own behavior the aimless wandering through the desert of their own patients? Now this is not intended to press the case for a rigidity of theory. I have noted through the years that the institutes most rigid in their theoretical orientation (e.g., the New York Psychoanalytic Institute) have least trouble with their students. In this type of setting the student is presented with *the one way*. This apparently creates little confusion for both the teacher and the student. But this skirts around the deeper issue of the meaning of the one way. In April 1966 the District of Columbia's highest court outlawed the routine imprisonment of chronic alcoholics. This decision, which I personally applaud, suddenly tossed into the area of psychotherapy a very basic ethical concept. The decision declared unanimously that chronic alcoholics could not be guilty of public drunkenness. The court stated that because a chronic alcoholic cannot control his drinking, he cannot have the intent necessary to be guilty of a drunk charge. While the short-range implications of such a decision are admirable, since they indicate treatment as the method of choice rather than imprisonment, there is the rather obvious shortage of treatment facilities, as well as the question of how effective these treatment facilities are. There is certainly no question about the difficulty of treating chronic alcoholics. A reporter for the *New York Times* (Samuels, 1966) described her impressions of the United States Public Health Service hospital in Lexington, Kentucky, the facility devoted to treating narcotics addicts. She quotes from Nyswander (1956), "In the long run, as with alcoholism, the patient's inner decision to stay off drugs determine's his cure." Recently *Science* printed a rather lengthy summary of the aftermath of a research project where live cancer cells were injected into hospitalized patients under circumstances in which the nature of their consent to the proceedings was exceedingly ambiguous (Langer, 1966). The subjects were twenty-two seriously ailing and debilitated patients in the Jewish Chronic Disease Hospital, Brooklyn, New York. The research concerned cancer immunology and is generally rated in the scientific community as among the most significant lines of research on malignant diseases. The researcher, Chester Southam, and his institution, Sloan-Kettering, are in the forefront of American medical science.

After almost two years and much publicity, the Regents of the University of the State of New York, who are responsible for licensing the medical profession, issued a report in which Southam and a collaborator were found guilty of unprofessional conduct and of fraud and deceit in the practice of medicine. Their licenses were suspended for one year and they were placed on probation. In the course of the review, the Regents and the medical grievance committee had to face two key questions. When is consent "informed," and how far may a physician exercise his authority when he is acting as an experimenter? In short, there was effort made to put some precision into the vague ethical concepts which now govern experimentation with human subjects. I don't want to discuss the case, but rather to note that the two men found guilty were only wandering through the same poorly defined wasteland as other researchers. The ethics of the experimental situation were never defined. The experimental zeal was admirable but the morality was never clarified.

My purpose here is not to remind us all of the long way we have to travel in treating many patients who are poorly motivated. Rather, it is to remind us again of the tremendous comingling of the individual's inner problem and the responsibility that society has placed upon psychotherapists to serve as public guardians. Have we then assumed Ernest Jones' vision of our service as high priests to stabilize this chaotic world? Are we ready to assume such service? Do we have the practical wisdom to accept such a task and are we too eager to prove ourselves? Are psychotherapists frustrated, secularized priests? If they are, they should not mask the role. Erich Fromm writes in a fashion that captures many readers. But is he an "old Aristotleian"? Does he really mask with his observations his definition of ideal human nature? As I understand him, goodness is to be healthy. Ideal human nature is to be healthy, happy and free. Everyone wants to be happy. The word "happy" is an absolute. The fulfillment of it is not an absolute. The manner of fulfillment involves flexibility. To paraphrase Oliver Wendell Holmes:

When John and Thomas talk together there is bound to be misunderstanding among the six of them. There is Thomas' ideal John, John's ideal John and the real John; they are all different, and the same is true of Thomas. Therefore, there is bound to be misunderstanding among the six.

Because of my concern about the misunderstanding. I have stressed, and will continue to stress, that the areas of confusion in the theory and practice of psychotherapy concern the ethic of the psychotherapist. No amount of search into the unconscious will find an ethic, for either psychotherapist or patient. The search will only show the road that one must travel. Martin Buber (1957) has said it far better than I can,

In a decisive hour, together with the patient entrusted to him and trusting in him . . . the therapist . . . has left the closed room of psychological treatment in which the analyst rules by means of his systematic and methodological superiority and has stepped forth with him into the air of the world where self is exposed to self. There, in the closed room where one probed and treated the isolated psyche according to the inclination of the self-encapsulated patient, the patient was referred to ever-deeper levels of his inwardness as to his proper world; here, outside, in the immediacy of one human standing over against another, the encapsulation must and can be broken through, and a transformed, healed relationship must and can be opened to the person who is sick in his relations to otherness—to the world of the other which he cannot remove into his soul.

Nowhere in the current ferment of training in psychotherapy do I find the emphasis on the ethic that should motivate the psychotherapist as he encourages both patient and himself to explore "relations to otherness." I believe that it is time for the emphasis to begin.

REFERENCES

Alexander, F., Eisenstein, S., and Grotjahn, M. (Eds.), *Psychoanalytic pioneers*. Basic Books, 1966. P. 616.

Buber, M. Dialogue between Martin Buber and Carl Rogers, April 18, 1957, Ann Arbor, Michigan, Unpublished.

Buber, M. *Pointing the way*: Collected essays. Ed. and trans. by Maurice S. Friedman. New York: Harper & Bros., 1957.

Frank, P., *Einstein, his life and times*. New York: Knopf, 1947. P. 284.

Frank, J. D. *Persuasion and healing*: *A comparative study of psychotherapy*. Baltimore: Johns Hopkins Press, 1961.

Friedman, M. *Existential psychotherapy and the image of man*. Unpublished paper, 1965.

Fromm, E. *The art of loving, beyond the chains of illusion, the heart of man*: *Its genius for good or evil*. New York: Harper, 1956.

Glass, B. *Science and ethical values*. Chapel Hill: University of North Carolina Press, 1965. P. 113.

Hill, L. B. On being rather than doing in group psychotherapy. *International Journal of Group Psychotherapy*, 8, 1958, 154–160.

Hora, T. Existential group psychotherapy. *American Journal of Psychotherapy*, 1959, 13, 83-92.

Jones, E. Some questions of ethics arising in relation to psychotherapy. *Dominion Medical Monthly*, 1910, 35, 17-22.

Jones, E. *What is psychoanalysis?* (1928). New edition, New York: International Universities Press, 1948. P. 126.

Jones, E. The God complex: The belief that one is God and the resulting character traits. *Essays in applied psychoanalysis*. London: Hogarth Press, 1951.

Langer, E. Human experimentation: New York verdict affirms patient's right. *Science*, 1966, 151, 663-666.

Lazarus, A. Group therapy of phobic disorders by systematic desensitization. *Journal of Abnormal and Social Psychology*, 1961, 63, 504–510.

Libby, H. E. Group therapy: An aid to the alcoholic. *Journal of the Maine Medical Association*, 57, 8–11.

Lyons, J. Existential psychotherapy: Fact, hope, fiction. *Journal of Abnormal and Social Psychology*, 1961, 62, 242–249.

Malone, T., Whitaker, C., Warkentin, J., and Felder, R. Rational and nonrational psychotherapy: A reply. *American Journal of Psychotherapy*, 1961, 15, 212–220.

Mullan, H. Status denial in group psychoanalysis. *Journal of Nervous and Mental Diseases*, 1955, 122, 345–352.

Nelson, B. Phenomenological psychiatry: Daseinsanalyze and American existential analysis. *Psychoanalysis and the Psychoanalytic Review*, 1961–1962, 48, 3–23.

Nyswander, M. *The drug addict as a patient.* New York: Grune & Stratton, 1956.

Reagan, M. New York Times Magazine, February 20, 1966.

Reik, T. *Ritual* (rev. ed.) New York: International Universities Press, 1958.

Reik, T. *Mystery on the mountain.* New York: Harper Bros., 1958.

Rogers, C. The necessary and sufficient conditions of therapeutic personality change. *Journal of Consulting Psychology*, 1957, 21, 95–103.

Rogers, C. The place of the person in the world of the behavioral sciences. *Personnel and Guidance Journal*, 1961, 39, 442–451.

Rosenbaum, M. The challenge of group psychoanalysis. *Psychoanalysis*, 1952, 1, 42–58.

Rosenbaum, M., and Hartley, E. A survey of prevailing practices and theory in group psychotherapy. *Annals of the 6th Inter-American Congress of Psychology*, Rio de Janeiro, Brazil, August, 1959.

Rosenbaum, M., and Hartley, E. A summary review of current practices of 92 group psychotherapists. *International Journal of Group Psychotherapy*, 1962, 12.

Samuels, G. A visit to narco. *New York Times*, April 10, 1966.

Schwartz, E. K. Group psychotherapy: The individual and the group. *Psychotherapy and Psychosomatics*, 1965, 13, 142–

149. 6th International Congress of Psychotherapy, London, 1964.

Shattan, S. P., Decamp, L., Fujii, E., Fross, G. G., and Wolff, R. J. Group treatment of conditionally discharged patients. *American Journal of Psychiatry*, 1966, 122, 798–805.

Szulc, Tad. *New York Times*, February 20, 1966.

Van Dusen, W. The theory and practice of existential analysis. *American Journal of Psychotherapy*, 1957, 11, 310–322.

Warkentin, J. Support through non-reassurance. *American Journal of Psychotherapy*, 1956, 10, 709–715.

Weber, M. *The Protestant ethic and the spirit of capitalism.* New York: Scribner, 1965.

Wexler, M. The structural problem in schizophrenia: Therapeutic implications. *International Journal of Psychoanalysis*, 32, 1951, 157–166.

Whitaker, C., and Malone, T. *The roots of psychotherapy.* New York: Blakiston Co., 1953.

Winnicot, D. W. Hate in the counter-transference. *International Journal of Psychoanalysis*, 1949, 30, 69–74.

Wolf, A., and Schwartz, E. Irrational psychotherapy: An appeal to unreason. *American Journal of Psychotherapy*, 1958–1959, 1–62.

Wolpe, J. *Psychotherapy by reciprocal inhibition.* Stanford University Press, 1958.

4

LEARNING THEORY: AN AID TO DYNAMIC THERAPEUTIC PRACTICE

THOMAS G. STAMPFL and DONALD J. LEVIS

WITHIN THE LAST decade, students of psychotherapy have witnessed a tremendous upsurge of interest in learning-oriented treatment procedures (Bandura, 1961; Grossberg, 1964). A major impetus for this development can be attributed in part to a serious questioning of the efficacy of conventional psychotherapeutic practice (Eysenck, 1952), to a growing need for an effective short-term treatment procedure, and to the actual development and application of promising learning theory techniques.

Examples of some of the learning positions which have emerged are Wolpe's (1958) reciprocal inhibition therapy based on Hull's (1943) theory of learning; Salter's (1949) conditioned reflex therapy based on Pavlovian conditioning principles; and Skinnerian operant techniques as reflected in the work of Ayllon (1963), Krasner (1958), and Lindsley (1956).

The promising potential for these learning techniques is believed to be related to the attempt of their originators to link the rationale of their techniques to theory and/or principles supported by controlled experimentation. Furthermore, a theoretical structure which reduces the major neurotic reactions into a series of conditioned responses provides a far more parsimonious explanation than traditional approaches, since it eliminates many of the surplus concepts inherent in the latter orientation.

The treatment techniques themselves are also appealing because of their simplicity and time-saving value. This latter factor perhaps can be attributed to the emphasis of behavioral therapists in stressing the need for manipulation of only one independent variable to account for treatment effectiveness. For example, Wolpe considers the main goal of treatment as the counter-conditioning of anxiety, while Salter emphasizes removal of inhibition, and the operant conditioners stress the effectiveness of appropriate positive or negative reinforcement contingencies.

Nevertheless, despite these desirable features, certain major disadvantages make the behavioral approach something less than palatable to many traditionally oriented clinicians. For one thing, the older techniques and theories are rejected in an almost contemptuous fashion. References to inner events and mysterious complexes are tinged by the behavioral therapists with an aura of ridicule. Concepts and methods, such as the role of the therapeutic relationship, transference, insight, and dynamic interpretations, are dismissed summarily without adequate experimental justification (Hilgard and Bower, 1966, pp. 294–295).

As a result of these radical departures from conventional orientation, training, and theory, many dynamically oriented clinicians are reluctant to see little more than gross oversimplifications on the part of the learning positions. Furthermore, considerable suspicion (Breger and McGaugh, 1965; Cooper, Gelder, and Marks, 1965; Marks and Gelder, 1965; Gelder, Marks, and Wolff, 1967) has surrounded the claims of effectiveness of these "new" treatment procedures.

Our thesis is that the acceptance of a learning theory position does not inherently result in the need to abandon all existing conventional conceptualizations and training techniques. On the contrary, it is maintained that the clinicians' existing training and experience will prove to be an invaluable aid in making this integration.

Although the purpose of this paper is to show how a fruitful marriage between behavioral and dynamically oriented theories might be effected, we do not intend simply to retranslate existing conventional treatment procedures into learning principles. This already has been accomplished by Shoben (1949) and Dollard and Miller (1950). Rather, an attempt will be made to analyze from a learning-theory position not only the etiology of patients' pathology, and also to provide the reader with a different solution from that of other behavioral therapists on how to remove or reduce this pathology. This different solution has developed into a new treatment procedure called Implosive Therapy (Stampfl, 1961, 1966; Levis, 1966; Stampfl and Levis, 1967a, b).

CONDITIONING PARADIGM

Before attempting to give a more detailed presentation of the learning relationships which are assumed to exist, it may prove helpful to present a brief outline of a few basic assumptions underlying this position. Perhaps this best can be accomplished by drawing a parallel between the avoidance conditioning model of the laboratory and human psychopathology. Aversive conditioning experiences which are assumed to be at the core of human psychopathology arise as a result of past specific experiences of punishment and pain, which confer strong emotional reactions to initially nonpunishing ("neutral") stimuli. When correlated with painful events, these essentially "neutral" stimuli acquire the potential to produce aversive emotional reactions in the absence of the original primary stimulation. The typical laboratory demonstration of this aversive conditioning involves the presentation of a nonaversive stimulus (e.g., a tone) for a designated interval (e.g., 5 seconds) followed by an inherently aversive stimulus such as electric shock. This latter stimulus is labeled an unconditioned stimulus (UCS). With sufficient pairings of the nonaversive stimuli with the UCS, these stimuli preceding the onset of the UCS acquire emotional properties similar to those elicited by the UCS. The emotional state elicited by the preceding stimuli (e.g., tone) is labeled fear or anxiety, and the stimuli producing the emotional state are designated as danger signals or conditioned stimuli (CS). This conditioned fear or anxiety state functions as a motivator of behavior, while any response of the subject which reduces or eliminates this fear state is assumed to serve as a reinforcer of behavior.[1] Active and passive avoidance learning are then obtainable by simply arranging the reinforcing contingencies in such a way that the subject's behavior enables him to terminate or avoid the emotionally conditioned danger signals. In the human situation, defensive mechanisms

---

[1] The adherence to a drive reduction interpretation of reinforcement is not an intrinsic requirement of the model. Other interpretations for the strengthening of the S-R bond conceivably could be substituted.

and symptomatology of the patient are viewed as the conditioned responses that remove or reduce the influx of conditioned anxiety. The similarity of this position with that of Freud's is apparent from the following quote:

Since we have reduced the development of anxiety to a response to situations of danger, we shall prefer to say that the symptoms are created in order to remove or rescue the ego from the situation of danger. If symptom formation is prevented, then the danger actually makes its appearance. . . . (Freud, 1936, p. 85)

EXPERIMENTAL EXTINCTION

Since psychopathology is here viewed as frequently being reflective of aversive conditioning experiences, how best might the conditioned anxiety be divested of its potential? One of the most reliable formulations coming out of the laboratory concerning this point is the original principle of Pavlov that presentation of the CS in the absence of the UCS will lead to the extinction of the learned response. In the words of Solomon, Kamin, and Wynn (1953),

the best way to produce extinction of the emotional response would be to arrange the situation in such a way that an extremely intense emotional reaction takes place in the presence of the CS. This would be tantamount to a reinstatement of the original acquisition situation, and since the US is not presented a big decremental effect should occur (p. 299).

There is much evidence indicating that this principle is a valid one, whether it is overt action or emotional states that have been learned (Miller, 1951; Hunt, Jernberg, and Brady, 1952; Black, 1958; Denny, Koons, and Mason, 1959; Knapp, 1965; Weinberger, 1965). Learning theorists have suggested models for psychotherapy which are based on this principle (Holland & Skinner, 1961; Kimble, 1961, p. 476).

A corollary to this principle is reflected in the experimental studies of Lowenfeld, Rubenfeld and Guthrie (1956) and Wall and Guthrie (1959), which indicate that the more clearly a subject perceives anxiety-eliciting stimuli followed by nonreinforcement, the more rapid is the extinction of the emotional response.

Essentially what is being said is that human psychopathology can result from the pairing of "neutral" stimuli with primary painful events. As a consequence of pairing, these "neutral" stimuli acquire aversive properties, which are then capable of secondarily motivating behavior. Defensive maneuvers and symptoms of the patient are believed to result from attempts on his part to avoid or terminate these conditioned stimuli that function as danger signals. The authors here propose that by implementing the simple and expedient laboratory model of preventing the subject's avoidance response (his symptoms) and directly forcing the patient to experience the avoided conditioned stimuli in the absence of primary reinforcement, the source of the secondary aversive motivation should extinguish.

Distinction between Primary and Secondary Reinforcement

Despite the theoretical simplicity of a direct extinction approach, and despite the fact that various writers have utilized theoretical formulations similar to the one employed here, the full implications of this approach have not been implemented by other therapeutic positions. Thus, Shoben (1949) objected to the possibility of having therapy merely consist of symbolizing acts which have been repressed. He said:

there is no indication of how such a procedure would accomplish anything more than the release of a flood of anxiety heretofore held in check. . . (p. 383).

Dollard and Miller (1950, p. 294) state that an awkward, stupid interpretation by the therapist which elicits strong fear is equivalent to a cruel therapist attaching a grid to the patient's chair and giving him a strong electric shock.

The dilemma above, is believed in part, to center around a misconception of what constitutes a primary and secondary reinforcer. Interestingly enough, learning theorists, speaking of animal experimentation, usually have little difficulty in making this distinction. The main difference noted is that, in principle, each exposure to a CS (secondary reinforcer) in the absence of the UCS (primary reinforcer) should result in some extinction effect for the reinforcing properties of the conditioned stimulus. With sufficient repetitions of the CS, complete extinction will occur (see Azrin and Holz, 1966). An aversive UCS with repetition should either increase in strength or at least maintain the fear-eliciting strength of stimulation correlated with it.

According to the present theoretical orientation, the aversive UCS must in principle involve a painful event, such as harmful, injurious, physical stimuli of the external environment, or painful deprivation states within the organism.

SEQUENTIAL CONDITIONED STIMULI

Since the treatment procedure advocated here is the direct exposure of conditioned aversive cues in the absence of the

UCS, both CS and UCS events occurring in the human situation are in need of further examination.

Both Hull (1943, pp. 204–206) and Mowrer (1960, pp. 37–38) indicate that primary stimulation tends to condition all (or a very large portion) of the total stimulation present at the time the conditioning occurs. Hull also is explicit in stating that the CS involved in even relatively "simple" conditioning situations is a most complex phenomenon.

It is clear that for the human S, other people may constitute important conditioned stimuli in the conditioning process. If one substitutes interaction with significant persons for the lights and buzzers used with laboratory animals, it can be assumed that in principle the conditioning and extinction processes are similar, if not identical.

Typical conditioning on the level of human experience frequently involves important differences from those of laboratory animal experiments, especially in respect to stimulus input. An example will help clarify what is meant. In an incident observed by the first author, two boys (twins) were "drawing" with stones various figures on the side of their father's new automobile, which was parked in the driveway next to their house. Their father appeared in the door of the house, uttered a roar, and rushed toward his sons picking up a shovel on the way. In an extremely menacing manner he approached the boys with the shovel upraised; he then swung the shovel several times but missed hitting them. He finally put down the shovel, took a firm grasp of their shoulders, and dragged them into the house. For an hour or so the boys were punished intermittently; the sounds were clearly audible, the father alternating between using a belt and using his hands. The cries and screams were of considerable intensity, and the crying did not completely subside until several hours later.

One of the outstanding differences between a traumatic event of this kind and that of the animal laboratory consists in the complex sequential stimulation which usually precedes and accompanies punishment in the human situation.

What is the conditioned stimulus in this description? Is it the complex proprioceptive, visual, and tactual stimulation associated with the boys picking up the stones, the complex stimulation correlated with their writing on the side of the car, seeing their father in the doorway, the auditory stimulation associated with his roar, the complex stimuli related to seeing him picking up the shovel, rushing down the steps, swinging the shovel, or being dragged into the house? Would the conditioned stimulus include the sight of the belt or hand of the father as it landed on various parts of the body, the preparatory responses made with the muscular tension accompanying them before being hit, the autonomic feedback from the emotional reactions, proprioceptive feedback from the postures adopted, feedback from the motor responses in struggling to escape, the auditory stimulation emanating from the father commenting on their worthlessness, or the auditory stimulation related to their cries and screams? Do context stimuli acquire aversive properties also? Are the sight of the clouds in the sky, the tunes they were humming, the thoughts they were having, the unique arrangement of the furniture in the rooms, the style of the automobile, etc., also elements of the conditioned stimulus?

If the unconditioned stimulus involves physical pain, then it is assumed that all the complex stimulation associated with the traumatic event functions as a unique stimulus pattern ordered sequentially in time that has acquired anxiety-eliciting properties. The CS is a complex patterned stimulus. An important point to note is that a stimulus element, such as the clouds in the sky, may have no anxiety-eliciting potential in itself, but adds to the total anxiety-eliciting potential of the stimulus pattern when it functions in context. Another point is that stimuli closely associated with pain are still conditioned aversive stimuli, not unconditioned stimuli. That is, the sight of the belt descending through the air and the sight of it on the body is an essentially "neutral" stimulus which acquires its aversiveness through its close association with pain. Furthermore, any cue relating to the traumatic event may activate or redintegrate other internal cues, and a stimulus pattern associated with a single traumatic event may have an associative linkage with the patterns representing other traumatic events.

It should be noted again that physical states of deprivation are considered as painful states in which the drive stimulation serves as the unconditioned stimulus. Conditioning to stimuli correlated with the deprivation state proceeds much like the preceding description of the boys punished by their father.

PRIMARY PROCESS THINKING

A learning orientation is also in agreement with dynamic theory in its emphasis on the role childhood experience plays in effecting current pathological behavior. Not only is it feasible that conditioning occurs to external cues in the environment, but it also is quite possible, as noted earlier, that the stimulus complex preceding punishment includes many internal cues. Some of these are referred to as images, thoughts, or desires. Since conditioning principles are believed to shape behavior from very early childhood, it is quite possible and also consistent with dynamic theory that the early conditioning experiences which occur prior to the full development of perceptual and discrimination skills might comprise CSs which would appear to an adult as exceedingly strange and bizarre. (In fact, the absence of logic in dreams may reflect these early conditioning experiences.) These early conditioning patterns could easily constitute what clinicians have labeled as primary process thinking. Fantasies and thought patterns involving, for example, cannibalistic, oral-incorporative behavior might simply be seen as the result of conditioning experiences which occur in the early oral-aggressive stage of development hypothesized by Freud. If these thought processes are paired with frustration, physical pain, or deprivation, they could acquire aversive properties and subsequently be avoided (repressed).

These analyses are consistent with the views of Kimble (1961), who states:

One advantage of the view that anxiety is a conditioned fear reaction is that it leads to the search, in the life history of the individual, for traumatic occasions which may provide the origin of anxiety. This has led to the emphasis on certain events in childhood which are often responsible for the development of anxiety. These events include some of the same episodes stressed by the psychoanalysts in their theory of psychosexual development, such as toilet training and the inhibition of infantile sexuality and aggression. One of the important points about such fears is that they are acquired before the child can talk. This appears to contribute to the difficulties encountered later on in trying to remember traumatic events which led to the development of anxiety (p. 474).

STIMULUS GENERALIZATION

It is not necessary that internal or external conditioned avoided stimuli directly represent past aversive events. Conditioned fear learned to one set of cues may transfer to other "neutral" stimuli. A learning analysis utilizes the concepts of stimulus generalization, higher order conditioning, response mediated generalization, and/or the principle of redintegration to account for this transfer. Simultaneously, these principles provide an explanation for displacement and symbolization as well. It might be noted that a spider which behaves like a cruel castrating mother, a horse that behaves like a father, and a snake that functions as a male phallus would by this fact represent considerable stimulus similarity to the aversive stimulus patterns they represent.

TREATMENT MODEL

Following the conditioning model presented above, a nonreinforcement position of extinction suggests itself as a possible treatment technique. The essential objective of the therapist is to expose the patient to the conditioned stimuli he is avoiding in the absence of any primary reinforcement. The introduction of these cues should lead to a marked increase in emotional responding (anxiety), which should decrease in intensity with each subsequent exposure. As the conditioned emotional response extinguishes, the symptomatic behavior based on the emotional state also should disappear. An outline of the method and rationale of this treament procedure will be presented in the following sections. Details of how the treatment technique is implemented can be found elsewhere (Stampfl & Levis, 1967a, b).

METHOD OF CS PRESENTATION

If the task at hand is to reproduce conditioned aversive cues to the patient, how best might this presentation be accomplished? Unfortunately, it is frequently difficult if not impossible to specify the conditioning (traumatic) events in the patient's life history with exact precision. However, it is usually possible for the trained clinician to locate "key" stimuli associated with the problem areas of the patient, and to formulate hypotheses as to the type of traumatic events which gave rise to the problem areas. In this respect, Alexander and French (1946,) stated that rapid recovery from neurotic reactions is likely to occur:

provided that the therapist is able to produce a replica of the traumatic situation with sufficient vividness to make it realistic. . . . And, what is most important, it makes no difference whether we deal with the effect of one acute traumatic situation or with the cumulative result of prolonged traumatic atmosphere of early family life. . . (p. 163).

The main point to be observed is that the clinician should approximate as closely as possible the hypothesized traumatic events, and reproduce the cues as realistically as possible. The use of imagery is thought to be a better mode of reproduction than the use of words alone.[2] In this respect, Erikson (1960) comments:

There is nothing profound in noting that language and words are highly abstract symbols and bear little or no physical resemblance to the objects, events, and relationships that they denote. A definition of awareness in terms of verbalization places a heavy burden upon the adequacy of language to reflect the richness of perceptual experiences and images (p. 280).

From a learning point of view, the "image" is considered

---

[2] In the present theoretical context "images" are considered hypothetical constructs. The experimental inducement of an image is attempted by verbal instructions and measured by such dependent variables as verbal report and psychophysiological measures.

to be a cue-producing response which is higher on a continuum of stimulus similarity than that of language alone.

RESISTANCE PHENOMENA

The therapist may well wonder just how it will be possible to have patients cooperate in a procedure which by its very nature is likely to elicit high degrees of anxiety. Exposure to cues that evoke anxiety should produce considerable resistance.

It is generally agreed that interpretations that are made too quickly or are too deep tend to interfere with the progress of therapy rather than to facilitate it. Fenichel (1945, p. 25) explicitly criticized those analysts who maintained that the patient should be "bombarded" with "deep interpretations." However, Fenichel's main objection is that the unprepared patient cannot experience the emotions appropriate to those interpretations. One question that might be asked is that even if procedures were developed which allowed the appropriate emotions to be experienced, would the patient then return for further sessions?

In the animal laboratory the experimenter extinguishes his animals' conditioned fear by simply presenting the CS repeatedly in the absence of primary reinforcement. Obviously, no effort would be made to insist that the animals attest to the validity of the stimulus used by providing symbols that confirm it. Rather the experimenter utilizes the elimination or reduction of the maladaptive behavior and/or the anxiety responses associated with it as criteria for the confirmation.

The human situation is obviously a different one; but if

the basic principle remained the same between the two situations, it would appear worthwhile to formulate it as an hypothesis and test it directly. Initially, one could apply the procedure to patients who displayed only mild degrees of personality disturbance. Clinical experience and experimental studies of this possibility have indicated that this is feasible. The main advantage of the procedure is that it tends to circumvent resistance and provide motivational factors for the continuation of therapy.

In order to achieve this objective, two levels of communication are maintained with the patient. One mode of communication is the ordinary conventional one employed by the therapist, i.e., the ordinary conversation which occurs between therapist and patient. In addition, whatever specialized techniques he might use can be included (e.g., free association, reciprocal inhibition). In another mode of communication, the patient closes his eyes and the therapist suggests scenes incorporating aversive stimuli to him. The critical difference between the fantasy scene directed by the therapist and the conventional interpretations made in dynamic therapies is that the attitudes and meanings of the patient in the suggested imaginal scene are to be accepted and believed only while the fantasy is in progress. Therefore, no inference that implications from these fantasies constitute an accurate reflection of the patient's behavior and mental life is made in the conversational mode of communication. The patient need not accept the attributes and meanings as existing within him in the real world. However, in the fantasy scenes the patient is asked to experience the attitudes and behavior as though they are real and apply to him even though they may not be true and the patient knows this. Of course, the patient may report that perhaps some of it is actually true. When he does this the therapist has an option to agree, disagree, or be neutral. The argument here is that "insight" may not be therapeutic (facilitate extinction) (see Hobbs, 1962; Heap and Sipprelle, 1966), although "insight" may well function to help motivate the individual to continue in therapy. Thus, the peculiar situation arises that the patient is asked to believe the implications for his behavior in one mode of communication, but need not accept them in the other mode.

Following the first session of this procedure, the patient may ask and the therapist might explain the rationale of the procedure emphasizing the need for anxiety reactions. The therapist might then give a simple explanation to the patient in terms of an avoidance model of conditioning. One aspect of the explanation is that in order to extinguish anxiety one must elicit anxiety. The patient thus is furnished with a rationale for the consistent efforts to develop scenes which are anxiety evoking. Much resistance seems to be overcome by this method.

One might ask, why does the patient return for more therapy sessions? It would seem that the attrition rate would be exceedingly high. Experience with the procedure indicates that this is not the case, probably because considerable relief and amelioration of symptomatology is experienced following a single session for many patients. This possibly provides the motivation for returning for additional sessions. As Alexander and French (1946) say,

In the course of one interview the patient may react with violent anxiety, weeping, rage attacks, and all sorts of emotional upheavals together with an acute exacerbation of his symptoms—only to achieve a feeling of tremendous relief before the end of the interview (p. 164).

HYPOTHESIZED STIMULUS PATTERNS

Another advantage of an avoidance-learning model of psychopathology is that, in addition to the usual problem areas treated by conventional therapeutic methods, it suggests additional CS patterns (cues related to problem areas) that can be introduced in treatment. Although consistent with much of psychodynamic theory, the present model tends to emphasize procedures at variance with common sense and traditional psychodynamic practice. The extent to which the following suggested patterns and procedures are effective is, of course, an essentially empirical matter.

The basic question that the therapist asks himself is simply: what is the patient avoiding? Whatever he concludes that the patient is avoiding can then be translated into its stimulus equivalents. On the basis of conditioning theory, it is assumed that these stimuli are capable of generating negative affect. The therapist attempts to reproduce an approximation of these stimulus equivalents so that the negative affect conditioned to these stimuli is elicited. The UCS is absent in this procedure, thereby setting the stage for a generalization of extinction effect to take place according to the Pavlovian principle of nonreinforcement.

The therapist is *not* merely attempting to induce anxiety, but also to reproduce those stimulus patterns with their secondary drive properties which are thought to provide the motivational force for the symptomatology. As will be pointed out later in this section, the symptom in some cases is an expression of this motivational process. In those cases, the therapist continues the process and extends it in order to obtain a greater extinction effect.

The following section of this paper will include examples of some of the stimulus patterns hypothesized to relate to the patient's symptomatology. Individual primary and secondary patterns will be considered in some detail. It should be remembered, however, that there is most likely an interrelated sequence of stimulus patterns present in the typical patient. Support for the relevance of the hypothesized cues will depend upon whether their presentation elicits anxiety. The greater the degree of anxiety elicited, the greater the support for continuing to present these cues.

Many of the cues involved in the patient's conditioning history can be identified as *symptom-contingent cues*. These are the situational or environmental cues which are highly correlated with the occurrence of the patient's symptom. They can be readily identified by analyzing the contingencies surrounding the occurrence of the symptom. As in the case of phobic reactions, the symptom-contingent cue might involve the sight of a tall building, the driving of a car, or being confined in a small enclosed space. These symptom-contingent cues can usually be reported by the patient.

The *hypothesized conditioned aversive* cues, which tend to be more completely avoided (repressed), stem in part from dynamic theory. Perhaps a clearer rationale of this type of cue can be obtained from the following learning analysis of the etiology of a few sample symptoms. Incorporated in the analysis are some of the hypothesized cues that might be presented to the patient in treatment.

DEPRESSION

A learning analysis of depressive reactions introduces an additional facet not emphasized in the preceding exposition. Two-process learning theory (Mowrer, 1960) assumes that stimuli coincident with positive reinforcement acquire the capacity to elicit a positive emotional response. The stimuli conditioned to elicit this response function as conditioned stimuli, and obey the same principles as those that govern conditioning in general. To say that an individual feels good emotionally, that there is a feeling of well-being and of security, is to say in learning terms that environmental and internal cues conditioned to produce positive affect are functioning. The elimination or reduction of these cues leads to a reduction in the degree of positive affect experienced. As will be seen, loss of positive affect in a conditioning sequence functions as a cue that elicits additional cues which generate negative emotional states representing feelings of guilt, worthlessness, and depressive reactions.

Two different conditioning analyses will be suggested although, once again, each patient must be considered individually.

A fairly typical sequence believed to occur in childhood is as follows: The child is tempted to engage in some tabooed or forbidden behavior. He yields to temptation and engages in the forbidden behavior, which is followed by his being apprehended, "caught," or "found out." The parent (the captor) may then continue along a verbal repetitive theme which focuses on the child's worthlessness and his guilt (e.g., "How could you do a thing like that?" "What kind of a child are you?" "What an awful, terrible thing to do!" "You should be ashamed of yourself!" "Don't you ever do a thing like that again." "You are a bad, bad child.") Direct physical punishment then follows, such as slapping, spanking, whipping, and/or punishment consisting of painful deprivation states, such as being sent to bed without supper and/or denial of privilege. Behavior on the part of the parent, which is equivalent in conditioning terms to "withdrawal of love," may accompany the sequence. If cues representing withdrawal of love have been previously conditioned, the child is punished additionally by the strong secondary aversive properties of these cues. Further, the cues maintain their aversiveness since they are correlated with primary reinforcers, painful physical punishment, and states of physical deprivation. Internal cues that represent the various segments of the chained conditioning events become a part of behavioral functioning and thus reflect the residue of past experience. Each segment can be reduced to its stimulus equivalents with complex visual, auditory, tactual, and proprioceptive properties. The activation of cues representing parental withdrawal of love through the process of generalization reduces, excludes, or inactivates those parental cues eliciting positive affect. The immediate result is loss of positive affect. However, the "withdrawal of love" cues are paired with noxious stimulation and acquire anxiety-arousing properties. According to this model, depression is then seen as resulting from a complex amalgam of loss of positive affect and anxiety arousal. The depressive reaction may be precipitated by present or past violations of the individual's system of values. In the absence of primarily noxious stimuli each exposure to the conditioned cues leads to some extinction of the depressive reactions. Nevertheless, most depressed patients are still avoiding some of the cues with a depression-producing potential.

One approach suggested by a learning analysis is to continue the depressive response while getting the patient to focus more closely on the internal cues producing the response (a procedure contrary to conventional therapeutic tactics). Then, scenes might be developed which concentrate on avoided cues. For example, the patient is directed to imagine that he has or is engaging in much "sinful" misbehavior. He is caught and accused by others (e.g., family, friends, police) and much comment on his great guilt and worthlessness is made. Cues relating to punishment are then presented. The secondary aversiveness of the cues should tend toward extinction.

A second model for depressive reactions is based on a conflict multiprocess approach-avoidance paradigm. The first stage consists of conditioned anxiety being associated to cues which precede punishment for the child's participation in some forbidden act. Continual primary and secondary punishment for such behavior not only heightens anxiety associated with the act, but especially in the case where completion of the taboo behavior culminates in positive reinforcement (e.g., sexual behavior), the punishment thwarts the desired approach response. The resulting conflict situation results in frustration, which leads to the enactment of aggressive behavior. If these overt aggressive tendencies on the part of the child are also punished, the overt aggressive behavior is then inhibited by anxiety arousal.

A partial solution to the dilemma above can be effected by channelizing the aggressive behavior primarily into internal cues (e.g., thoughts, images, ruminations) which involve aggressive fantasies toward the punishing agent. However, if the punishing agent is a source of considerable positive primary and secondary reinforcement (e.g., the mother who provides a protective, nurturant role), the aggressive internalized cues expressed by the child toward this figure will, in turn, decrease the strength of past positively conditioned internalized cues (e.g., thoughts or images of the mother as a supportive, "loving" figure).

In order not to diminish the positive reinforcement associated with the child's conceptualization of the punishing agent and to reduce additional secondary anxiety (guilt) over expressing the internal aggressive cues (thoughts), the aggressive fantasies and responses associated with aggressive behavior are avoided (suppressed). This additional internalization of the conditioned aggressive cues are believed to involve responses directly antagonistic to overt aggressive responses. The resulting state is experienced as depression. Furthermore, the self-punishing effects of the depressive reaction also help reduce secondary anxiety. This latter response category may also be continually positively reinforced since it usually elicits considerable secondary gain.

In order to decondition the avoided cues believed operating in this model, it is suggested that scenes including strong aggressive impulses directed toward important nurturant figures be developed, emphasizing feelings of "guilt" being elicited for the aggressive acts which, in turn, are followed by the conditioned cues associated with punishment.

AGGRESSION

The assumption is made that unconditioned emotional responses to unconditioned (primary) painful stimulation include differentiable autonomic reactions, which may be labeled as anxiety in the one case and anger in the other (Ax, 1953). Anxiety reactions are believed to be elicited when painful stimulation involving physical injury to body tissue occurs; while anger reactions are believed to be elicited when unconditioned painful stimulation involving the omission of primary positive reinforcement following prior positive reinforcement experience occurs. The anger response is then associated with stimuli surrounding the thwarting or omission of the positive reinforcement (the frustrating situation). Overt aggressive responses elicited by the emotional response of anger become conditioned when they terminate the frustrating conditioned and/or unconditioned stimuli responsible for the painful stimulation.

In the human situation, the learned aggressive reactions and the feedback arising from the anger response frequently become punished. In this case, as noted in our second model of depression, the aggressive reaction arising from anger may be displaced or avoided by means of other instrumental responses, since the response correlated stimulation of the aggressive act becomes anxiety arousing.

Repeated elicitation of the anger reaction to frustration stimuli in the absence of primary reinforcement (physical state of deprivation) should lead to the extinction or reduction of the anxiety response, and to a reduction of conditioned stimuli directly eliciting the anger reaction.

Suggested scenes to present in the area would center around the expression of anger, hostility, and aggression by the patient toward parental, sibling, spouse, or other significant figures in his life.

Various degrees of bodily injury of the victim should be suggested, including complete body mutilation and death of the victim. For example, diabolical injury and murder involving decapitation, slashing significant figures to pieces, castrating and drowning the victim, should result in an appreciable diminution of the conditioned cues associated with this response category.

ACCEPTANCE OF CONSCIENCE

The cues conditioned in this category are based on Mowrer's (1966) integrity therapy reinterpreted in terms of learning principles. Briefly, considerable aversive conditioning may occur to behavior that appears to reflect the notion of "integrity" or morally "honest" behavior. Consider a child who reveals (confesses) the commission of forbidden (previously punished) behavior to his parents. Frequently this verbal acknowledgment is accompanied by stimulus patterns comprising parental pressure to "own up" to the misbehavior. When the child admits to his misbehavior he may then be punished. The act of confessing, feeling "responsible" and "bad," then becomes a complex conditioned cue with anxiety-eliciting properties. Thus, cues associated with these states are subsequently avoided (Fenichel, pp. 164–166).

To extinguish these avoided cues, scenes are portrayed in which the patient confesses, admits, and is asked to believe that he is responsible and guilty for all sins and wrongdoings throughout his life. The surroundings may involve a court room scene with all the patient's family and loved ones present. After his confession he is punished by the court (e.g., hanging, electric chair) until he dies. When it is presumed that it might be appropriate and effective, the therapist can direct the patient to imagine himself before God, where the theme is essentially repeated with God condemning him to eternal suffering.

Inferiority Feelings

A number of patients present a variety of complaints more or less centering around feelings of inferiority. These include feelings of inadequacy, cowardice, being a failure, lack of physical beauty or physical strength and abilities.

The therapist may begin by suggesting scenes related to the complaint; the patient is pictured as a completely inferior person who has "zero" personality resources and abilities. It is suggested in various scenes that although the patient strives with great effort, his almost total lack of ability (he feels inferior because he is inferior) prevents him from accomplishing anything. Essentially the same procedure is followed with complaints of lack of physical attractiveness. The individual is instructed to picture himself as an extremely ugly person. Reactions to the individual from the other significant individuals in his life is proportionate to the ugliness. Of course, the therapist may attempt to trace the conditioning events in the individual's past history that have led to the feelings of inferiority.

The theoretical basis for this procedure is that it may be true enough that the patient does suffer from feelings of inferiority or inadequacy, but that he also is constantly striving to avoid them in daily life. Even the patient's complaint to the therapist is tinged with qualities of avoidance. The patient indirectly is soliciting reassurance from the therapist that it is not true, that he is not *really* inferior, and that the therapist will tell him so. When the therapist asks him to close his eyes and see himself very vividly and clearly as an absolutely inferior person, that this is really true, the patient frequently tends to avoid by pointing out his strong points. If the therapist then attempts to neutralize the objections so that the individual indeed experiences himself as completely inferior in the context of the hypothetical conditioning experiences that led to the feelings, then cues associated with this state, if correctly hypothesized, should extinguish.

Additional stimulus categories including punishment, sexual material, primal and Oedipal scenes, scenes of fellatio, homosexuality, oral and anal material, bodily injury, feelings of loss of control, cues associated with strangeness and suddenness, autonomic and central nervous system reactivity, can also be integrated into the scenes when they fit the particular dynamics of the case. For a more complete description of the categories above see Stampfl and Levis, 1967a.

CONCLUSION

Although it may appear on occasion that by introducing instructions to imagine these scenes the therapist is punishing the patient for behavior represented in immediately preceding scenes, it should be remembered that the entire chain of stimuli functions only as secondarily aversive stimuli, since images, thoughts, or words do not result in physical injury. Furthermore, the conditioned negative affect elicited by the total chained stimulus complex is considered responsible for the patient's mental turmoil and for providing the motivating source for symptom development and perpetuation. Repeated elicitation of the avoided chained complexes should result in marked anxiety reduction related to these stimuli through the principle of extinction.

The effectiveness of the approach above is in the last analysis an empirical matter. Some initial experimental support, however, already has been obtained (see Hogan, 1966; Kirchner and Hogan, 1966; Hogan and Kirchner, 1967; Levis and Carrera, 1967). Nevertheless, considerable caution should be maintained about the effectiveness of any treatment procedure until sufficient systematic experimental work with adequate follow-up data is completed.

REFERENCES

Alexander, F., and French, T. M. *Psychoanalytic therapy*. New York: Ronald Press, 1964.

Ax, A. F. The physiological differentiation between fear and anger in humans. *Psychosomatic Medicine*, 1953, 15, 433–442.

Ayllon, T. Intensive treatment of psychotic behavior by stimulus satiation and food reinforcement. *Behavior Research and Therapy*, 1963, 1, 53–61.

Azrin, N. H., and Holz, W. C. Punishment. In W. K. Honig's (Ed.), *Operant behavior: Areas of research and application.* New York: Appleton-Century-Crofts, 1966.

Bandura, A. Psychotherapy as a learning process. *Psychological Bulletin*, 1961, 58, 143–157.

Black, A. H. The extinction of avoidance responses under curare. *Journal of Comparative and Physiological Psychology*, 1958, 51, 519–524.

Breger, L., and McGaugh, J. L. Critique and reformulation of "Learning-Theory" approaches to psychotherapy and neurosis. *Psychological Bulletin*, 1965, 63, 338–358.

Cooper, J. E., Gelder, M. G., and Marks, I. M. Results of behavior therapy in 77 psychiatric patients. *British Medical Journal*, 1965, 1, 1222–1225.

Eriksen, C. W. The case for perceptual defense. *Psychological Review*, 1960, 67, 279–300.

Eysenck, H. J. The effects of psychotherapy: An evaluation. *Journal of Consulting Psychology*, 1952, 16, 319–324.

Denny, M. R., Koons, P. B., and Mason, J. E. Extinction of avoidance as a function of the escape situation. *Journal of Comparative and Physiological Psychology*, 1959, 52, 212–214.

Dollard, J., and Miller, N. E. *Personality and psychotherapy.* New York: McGraw-Hill, 1950.

Fenichel, O. *The psychoanalytic theory of neurosis.* New York: Norton, 1945.

Freud, S. *The problem of anxiety.* (H. A. Bunker, Trans.) New York: Psychoanalytic Quarterly Press and W. W. Norton & Co., 1936.

Gelder, M. G., Marks, I. M., and Wolff, H. H. Desensitization and psychotherapy in the treatment of phobic states: A controlled inquiry. *British Journal of Psychiatry*, 1967, 113, 53–73.

Grossberg, J. M. Behavior therapy: A review. *Psychological Bulletin*, 1964, 62, 73–88.

Heap, R. F., and Sipprelle, C. N. Extinction as a function of insight. *Psychotherapy: Theory, Research, and Practice*, 1966, 3, 81–84.

Hilgard, E. H., and Bower, G. H. *Theories of learning*. New York: Appleton-Century-Crofts, 1966.

Hobbs, N. Sources of gain in psychotherapy. *American Psychologist*, 1962, 17, 741–747.

Hogan, R. A. Implosive therapy in the short term treatment of psychotics. *Psychotherapy: Theory, Research, and Practice*, 1966, 3, 25–31.

Hogan, R. A., and Kirchner, J. H. A preliminary report of the extinction of learned fears via short term implosive therapy. *Journal of Abnormal Psychology*, 1967, 72, 106–109.

Holland, J. G., and Skinner, B. F. *The analysis of behavior*. New York: McGraw-Hill, 1961.

Hull, C. L. *Principles of behavior*. New York: Appleton-Century-Crofts, 1943.

Hunt, H. F., Jernberg, P., and Brady, J. V. The effect of electroconvulsive shock (E.C.S.) on a conditioned emotional response: The effects of post-E.C.S. extinction on the reappearance of the response. *Journal of Comparative and Physiological Psychology*, 1952, 45, 589–599.

Kimble, G. A. Hilgard & Marquis' *Conditioning and learning*. New York: Appleton-Century-Crofts, 1961.

Kirchner, J. H., and Hogan, R. A. The therapist variable in the implosion of phobias. *Psychotherapy: Theory, Research, and Practice*, 1966, 3, 102–104.

Knapp, R. K. Acquisition and extinction of avoidance with similar and different shock and escape situations. *Journal of*

Comparative and Physiological Psychology, 1965, 60, 272–273.

Krasner, L. Studies of the conditioning of verbal behavior. *Psychological Bulletin*, 1958, 55, 148–170.

Levis, D. J. Implosive therapy, Part II: The subhuman analogue, the strategy, and the technique. In S. G. Armitage (Ed.), *Behavioral modification techniques in the treatment of emotional disorders*. Battle Creek, Michigan: V.A. Publication, 22–37, 1966.

Levis, D. J., and Carrera, R. N. Effects of 10 hours of implosive therapy in the treatment of outpatients: A preliminary report. *Journal of Abnormal Psychology*, 1967, 72, 504–508.

Lindsley, O. R. Operant conditioning methods applied to research in chronic schizophrenia. *Psychiatric Research Reports*, 1956, 5, 118–138.

Lowenfeld, J., Rubenfeld, S., and Guthrie, G. M. Verbal inhibition in subception. *Journal of General Psychology*, 1956, 54, 171–176.

Marks, I. M., and Gelder, M. G. A controlled retrospective study of behavior therapy in phobic patients. *British Journal of Psychiatry*, 1965, 111, 561–573.

Miller, N. E. Learnable drives and rewards in S. S. Stevens (Ed.), *Handbook of experimental psychology*. New York: Wiley, 1951.

Mowrer, O. H. *Learning theory and behavior*. New York: Wiley, 1960.

Mowrer, O. H. Integrity therapy: A self-help approach. *Psychotherapy: Theory, Research, and Practice*, 1966, 3, 114–119.

Salter, A. *Conditioned reflex therapy*. New York: Farrar, Straus, 1949.

Shoben, E. J. Psychotherapy as a problem in learning theory. *Psychological Bulletin*, 1949, 46, 366–392.

Solomon, R. L., Kamin, L. J., and Wynne, L. C. Traumatic avoidance learning: The outcomes of several extinction procedures with dogs. *Journal of Abnormal and Social Psychology*, 1953, 48, 291–302.

Stampfl, T. G. Implosive therapy: A learning theory derived psychodynamic therapeutic technique, 1961. In R. C. La Barba & O. B. Dent (Ed.), *Critical issues in clinical psychology*. New York: Academic Press, 1967 (in press).

Stampfl, T. G. Implosive therapy, Part I: The theory. In S. G. Armitage (Ed.), *Behavioral modification techniques in the treatment of emotional disorders*. Battle Creek, Michigan: V.A. Publication, 12–21, 1966.

Stampfl, T. G., and Levis, D. J. The essentials of implosive therapy: A learning theory based psychodynamic behavioral therapy. *Journal of Abnormal Psychology*, 1967a, 72, 496–503.

Stampfl, T. G., and Levis, D. J. Implosive therapy. In R. M. Jurjevich (Ed.), *Handbook of direct and behavior psychotherapies*. Prentice-Hall: Englewood Cliffs, N.J. (in press).

Wall, H. N., and Guthrie, G. M. Extinction of responses to subceived stimuli. *Journal of General Psychology*, 1920, 3, 1–14.

Weinberger, N. M. Effects of detainment on extinction of avoidance responses. *Journal of Comparative and Physiological Psychology*, 1965, 60, 135–138.

Wolpe, J. *Psychotherapy by reciprocal inhibition*. Stanford: Stanford University Press, 1958.

5

A GRID MODEL FOR
THEORY AND RESEARCH IN
THE PSYCHOTHERAPIES

DONALD J. KIESLER

It is intriguing to confront the so-called three forces of psychology, each of which deals with the same issue in the preceding chapters of this volume. Psychoanalysis, behavior therapy, and existentialism seem at the very least to be very strange bedfellows. The underlying philosophies are echoed in semantic differences to the point where one wonders if in fact the various contributors are addressing the same issue.

Semantic idiosyncrasy is one matter. Theoretical and research confusion is another and more serious concern. As I have tried to argue (Kiesler, 1966), we can no longer tolerate this confusion either in our theoretical speculations or in our research designs regarding psychotherapy. The contributions of this volume provide some evidence that we are beginning at last to move in a more sensible direction.

Within the context of the presentations in this volume this chapter will extend the methodological and conceptual concerns of the author's previous work. We will attempt to present a grid-paradigm that exemplifies theorizing and research regarding psychotherapy and which should move us forward in our scientific knowledge of how behavior changes in a one-to-one "psychotherapy" situation.

It seems important first to clarify a point about psychotherapy research. This concerns the issue of psychotherapy as art or science. The "third force," as evidenced by the existential position (Chapter 3), seems to be heaping coals under this cauldron of confusion. The position presented here draws heavily from what this author believes are the most underrated volumes on psychotherapy in the last decade (Phillips, 1956).

ART VS. SCIENCE IN PSYCHOTHERAPY

When people attempt to study psychotherapy they are often baffled by its complexity. How can they begin to understand such a highly subjective, individualistic event? Patients are similar in many ways but the differences seem to be more important. The sequence of therapy events appear to be unique for a given interaction, and probably will never again occur in the same manner. As a result, therapy represents very much "playing it by ear," "flying by the seat of one's pants," and the like. It's an "unidentified technique applied to unspecified problems with unpredictable outcomes" (Raimy, 1950). As teachers of psychotherapy we are asked "What should I do with such-and-such a patient?" We reply, "It depends!"

How can we research or even theorize about such a phenomenon? The unique event is paramount! Any generality that makes some sense may be contradicted completely by a particular case. The existentialists tell us that this is the crux of the matter. This is the way it is and must be. This is what the therapist deals with, and if he doesn't, he has "missed the boat." As Rosenbaum points out in this volume, "The oneness of the individual is not to be denied. . . . All that it [psychotherapy] can finally do is emphasize the uniqueness of man so that he may move forward to face the paradoxes, absurdity, and often the despair of life." This emphasis seems to banish forever a science of psychotherapy, as seems to be evident from the lack of emphasis on technique found in existential writings. This is pointed out by Strupp in Chapter 2.

The extreme of this position is maintained by Colby (1964): ". . . psychotherapy is not a science, is not even an applied science and by its nature can never become either of these" (p. 348). Colby then proceeds to quote a previous paper of his: "It is a practical art, a craft like agriculture, or medicine, or wine-making in which an artisan relies on an incomplete, fragmentary body of knowledge and empirically established rules traditionally passed on from master to apprentice. The artisan lacks a systematic, thoroughly tested or even well-defined set of explanatory principles. His scraps of knowledge are not simply applied to an individual case but *interpreted* for each individual case in accordance with the artisan's judgment and intuition. He looks to science for help, not to make him an applied scientist, which cannot be done anyway—but to elucidate acute difficulties in the art"

118   *Donald J. Kiesler*

(Colby, 1962, p. 95). He continues: "Skillful arts are learned mainly in apprenticeships because the rules governing performance cannot be specified. One learns to do therapy by following expert examples and thereby picks up the hidden decision rules of therapeutic algorithms and heuristics. Not only does the transmission of skills involve tacit knowing . . . but much of the process of therapy takes place outside the focal awareness of the participants. When patient and therapist disagree as to what happened in therapy, when experts disagree as to what is crucial in therapy, it may be that none of them is right since none of them can articulate tacit knowledge" (p. 350).

In light of this, one must ask, What is psychotherapy theory and research all about? how can one specify, manipulate, or measure tacit variables? Each case not only involves tacit interaction but is inextricably unique, special, never to happen again! If this is the case, then obviously we cannot be dealing with science here, since there is no level of generality apparent or possible.

Is this the state of affairs with which we must live? It is the author's opinion that this trend of thinking is confused, obfuscating the science–art distinction and mirroring the subtle influence of the idiographic–nomothetic controversy. Phillips (1956) has made some of these same points very well and we quote him at some length:

Herein lies a real and lasting lesson for the clinician. He, too, tends to pile one discrete fact on another (most noticeably when he purports to deal with the whole person without theoretical guidance), and fails to reach a conceptual level providing for the economical interpretation of successive cases. One often hears clinicians say, "Why, each person is so *different* from others that no generalizations are possible," until he almost despairs of ever reaching a level of discourse with them that would permit discussion of scientific problems concerning human beings.

Too, herein may lie the idiographic-nomothetic controversy in another of its chameleonlike colorations. Once we reach a conceptual level in dealing with a case (or cases), we are on firmer and higher ground, we can see over the terrain, and can place successive problems, cases, or whatnot in perspective. Failure to reach this level of consideration, however, leaves one grappling with problems of the individual vs. the group, with the impulse to consider each successive case as different from the previous ones, and with the piling up of thousands of un-digested facts that fit no pattern or conceptual mold (pp. 82–83).

. . . uniqueness is a matter of degree; it is not an all-or-none characteristic. There is no notion operationally or conceptually of uniqueness as a total difference that makes sense. Things and people are unique only to a degree, and always in terms of the familiarity one has with what one encounters in such people and things.

Now if the variables used to describe a person are not, them-selves, different, the clinician would argue, then their arrange-ment, their *patterning* is different from one person to another, to such an extent that no two ever have *exactly* the same pattern. It would be argued that this is the domain, par excellence, of the clinician, that it is only he with his perceptive powers geared as they are who can discern the individuality of a single person. This brings to light a *procedural* difference between idiographic and nomothetic study, but this procedural difference is not a methodological one.

The clinician in interviews, in therapy, or in the usual situa-tions where he functions, *does not limit his choice of data in ad-vance as explicitly and as rigidly* as does the researcher who is investigating a collection of people with regard to an hypothesis. The clinician proceeds with an "open" classification (or hy-pothesis) system as he interacts with a client; the nomothetic research by design and by intention limits the data he will accept and thus can be said to operate with a limited or "closed" system of variables. Now, both nomothetist and clinician *infer* from the data they discern (observe, record) certain *conceptualizations* (descriptions, additional hypotheses, predictions, theories) regarding the client (subject, patient) to the end that summary statements, theories, hypotheses, may be made, confirmed, rejected, and so on. Thus the *procedures* of the clinician and of the actuarial researcher differ—but their *methods* of inferring from data to theory are identical" (p. 68).

Our position is that the idiographic–nomothetic controversy is spurious. We submit that the two are aspects of the same method of scientific inference, that they represent different emphases at different points in the scientific enterprise; and that it is fundamentally irrelevant whether one is dealing with one case or many cases as to the *course of inference* from data to theory (or to conceptualization) (p. 67).

As we have shown, Allport and nearly all clinicians tend to emphasize strongly the quality of uniqueness in the individual case or individual event. This matter seems to the writer to have been emphasized out of all proportion both for the understanding of the individual case and for the purpose of general scientific understanding. Reichenbach's position is to the point again: "In spite of this extension of general relationships, explanation does not deprive the individual event of its uniqueness. Every physical event is unique; there are no two events which are completely alike. Yet different events can very well belong to the same class. The same is true for historical events; although each of them is unique, historical events may very well be incorporated into classes. No two weather situations are identical; but they may very well be of a type usually followed by a thunderstorm. . . . Both in the physical and in the social sciences, classification of unique situations according to suitable characteristics leads to general laws. And the logic of explanation is the same for historical and for physical events; historical explanation, like physical explanation, consists in showing that the individual occurrence is of a pattern for which a general relationship can be established (pp. 74–75).

To summarize Phillips' position regarding psychotherapy, generalization *is* possible when dealing with individual therapy cases. Uniqueness is a matter of degree, inasmuch as patients can be characterized at different levels of the same dimensions. The patterning of their behavior along these dimensions may be different from patient to patient, but this is a procedural problem and does not contradict the scientific process. Methodologically, one is utilizing the same process whether dealing with individual cases or groups of cases. The important conceptual process lies in *inferring* from the data the generalities that may be present. Hence, it is irrelevant whether one is dealing with one patient or many patients insofar as the "course of inference" from data to theory is concerned. Classification of (inferences from) unique situations in psychotherapy according to suitable characteristics leads to general laws. Explanation, for the therapist as well as for any other scientist, consists in showing that the individual patient occurrences are of a pattern for which a general relationship can be established.

Phillip's position seems to bear crucially on the argument that psychotherapy is the art of the unique case. In its applied setting psychotherapy is certainly that. But even there it can be more. It can be an applied science of behavior modification. For, having inferred generalities from interactions with individual patients, the therapist can then apply and evaluate these hypotheses with other individual patients. This permits a fruitful chain of conceptual events, inference of hypotheses from individual cases, and application and verification of these hypotheses on subsequent cases.

Colby's thinking about psychotherapy as an art can become loose, undisciplined, and inexplicit, particularly if he incorrectly accepts the notion that since each case is unique, there can be no generality. Actually psychotherapy artisans do not always talk as Colby implies. They at times describe their unique cases as being "obsessive-compulsives" or "actor-outers" or "autistic" and the like, implying that more general labels are useful in their conceptualization and treatment of cases. The conclusion has to be that often cases are in some sense alike and the equivalences are crucial (and here we have the beginnings of science); but that cases are also unique and the idiosyncrasies are pivotal (and here we have the artisanship). Psychotherapy, or behavior modification is both a science and an art, depending upon one's focus.

Perhaps clinicians, trapped by this idiographic philosophy, have become lackadaisical, satisfied with inexplicit and loose conceptualizations. As Strupp states in Chapter 2: "there is no guarantee that an unperceptive practitioner following the existential viewpoint can successfully avoid the danger of getting lost in the vagaries of the patient's idiosyncratic experience." Perhaps the time has come not to permit clinicians to remain vague behind the shield of their "unique" cases. If one does different things with different kinds of cases, perhaps some hard and careful self-observation will be able to explicate the different therapist behaviors as well as the corresponding patient cues which elicit these different behaviors. This kind of careful clinical inference explicitly expressed will be very useful fodder for our theoretical mills. It seems that much of the psychotherapy literature, particularly since H. S. Sullivan, indicates that this trend is operative. The second part of this chapter will emphasize further that we do not need theories of behavior modification for patients as some kind of mystical homogeneous mass, or for the individual unique case (which is impossible). Rather we need the theories for something like "obsessive-compulsives," "hysterics," "depressives," "process schizophrenics," etc. Idiography both in psychotherapy and science has a place only as a point of observation for inferential operations. It is these inferences that take us away from the single case to more general phenomena which are amenable to theoretical manipulation.

Finally, Phillips makes an additional point that this author would like to underscore since it is the heart of the grid-model to be presented. In order to make theoretical and research progress we must move away from the completely unique event, just as we must move away from the completely general event. It is relatively useless to continue to focus on "the psychotherapy" (therapist uniformity assumption) with "the patient" (patient uniformity assumption) leading to "the therapeutic change" (outcome uniformity assumption). As this author has argued ". . . it would seem quite essential and useful to bury these uniformity myths once and for all. Until our designs can incorporate relevant patient variables and crucial therapist dimensions—so that one can assess which therapist behaviors are more effective with which type of patients—we will continue to perpetuate confusion. Psychotherapy research must come to grips with the need for factorial designs . . . wherein different types of patients are assigned to different types of therapists and/or therapy, so that one can begin to discover the parameters needed to fill in a meaningful paradigm for psychotherapy" (Kiesler, 1966, p. 113).

In light of this it is informative to hear Phillips' similar comments:

The idiographic position also entails and promotes a view of man that partially appears in long-term psychoanalytic practices. Here the emphasis is on pursuing idiosyncratic elements without reference to economy, to general lawfulness in behavior, or to knowledge in other areas that can be brought to bear on clinical problems. On the other hand, many counseling practices derive from and entail views of behavior that are not as constructive as they might be and that are too closely tied to nomothetic knowledge that does not go beyond test results, and which fails to come to grips as much as it might with the problems people concretely experience in daily living.

There is need for a view of psychotherapy, of psychological change, and of related personality considerations that can lie intermediate, in time and place and effort, and in scientific testability, between these two extremes; a view that can develop a rationale supporting such intermediate practices based on general knowledge in the behavioral and social sciences. The idiographic method applied to clinical work leads to impasses, to impractical dead-ends, to a boring-in for the sake of itself, and to scientific views that are low on usefulness and heuristic promise. The nomothetic view untempered and unextended by formulations such as conflict theory can trail off into inconsequentiality and superficiality. Both of these relatively unproductive extremes are to be avoided (pp. 88–89).

It is the purpose of the next section to extend the author's thinking in greater detail regarding a model of psychotherapy or behavior modification that would be useful for current theoreticians to consider and incorporate. The hope is that this attempt at specification will lead others to conceptualize explicitly in a similar manner, so that their theoretical products will be explicitly stated and restricted, and hence more susceptible of empirical verification.

CURRENT THEORETICAL MODELS OF PSYCHOTHERAPY

One of the major themes of the current author's previous article (Kiesler, 1966) was that present theoretical formulations regarding psychotherapy are woefully inadequate, primarily because they do not incorporate both patient and therapist individual differences into their formulations—in other words, are too general and inexplicit (hence opening the way for clinicians to hide behind the philosophy of the unique case). As Strupp states in Chapter 2, "It was assumed that any analyst, so long as he was properly trained, would follow Freud's technique in essential respects, and that individual differences among therapists were negligible. In other words, therapists were regarded as interchangeable units." In reviewing Freudian, Rogerian, and behavior therapy formulations Kiesler (1966) stated:

Each of the three theoretical positions has failed to specify exactly what the independent or dependent variables are. None has methodically dealt with the problems of the quality or quantity of outcome expected from the respective therapeutic interventions, or of differential outcome for different kinds of patients. None has dealt with the sampling and other methodological considerations which, remaining unspecified, make it impossible to design a test of present constructs (p. 121).

In summary, the basic deficiencies in prevailing theoretical formulations are that they perpetuate and do not attack the Uniformity Myths described in the previous section; do not explicitly deal with the problem of confounding variables; and do not specify the network of independent, dependent, and confounding variables in sufficient enough detail to permit researchers to solve sampling and other methodological problems. In view of these considerations, it seems evident that our formulations about psychotherapy contain serious inadequacies. Until our present theories are brought up to date by being made more comprehensive and by spelling out in much detail the variables of the theoretical paradigm—or until new formulations are introduced which meet the same requirements—it seems that psychotherapy investigators must continue to make arbitrary decisions regarding these parameters, or attempt to fill in the paradigm themselves with much exhaustive but necessary prior methodological research (pp. 125–126).

The author considered these deficiencies in much detail in his previous presentation. The major points only will be emphasized here and accentuated further by observations of other authors.

What is the *independent variable* in these theoretical systems? Generally, it seems clear that the independent variable in psychotherapy has to lie somewhere in the therapist and his behavior.

Just as clearly, it is evident from the above that present formulations have not specified in sufficient detail what these independent variables are: For analytical therapy it lies somewhere among a matrix of therapist attitudinal, technique, and personality factors (e.g., ambiguity, interpretation, personal maturity). For Rogerian therapy it lies somewhere in the interactional matrix of three therapist conditions or attitudes (positive regard, empathic understanding, and congruence). For behavior therapy it falls somewhere in the communication by the therapist of specific unlearning procedures. Obviously, more critical thinking needs to be given to the exact delineation of the therapist variable or variables instrumental in effecting patient change (Kiesler, 1966, p. 128.)

Ford and Urban (1963) comment on the same deficiency:

Therapy theorists have written extensively about the 'dynamics of behavior'—how behavior works, the patterns in which certain responses occur, the way one kind of response very often follows another, and how certain patterns and sequences of responses are typical of disordered behavior. When the issue of technique arises, however, as a group they have had far less to say. Problems of technique have been discussed in terms of the *effects* to be achieved, rather than in terms of the *procedures* to be used to achieve such effects. Frequently, therapists say that anxiety should be reduced, without any specification of how it can be done, or what situational events are to be manipulated to achieve the reduction. *Some arranging of situational events is always implied, since a therapist is considered essential in all ten systems!* (pp. 666–667).

Some (systems) propose that free association can serve these purposes (Freud, Dollard and Miller, Horney); others suggest that the therapist conduct an inquiry to provoke the responses he wishes to have occur (Adler, Sullivan, Wolpe); still others propose that an effective relationship is the essential requirement (Rank, Rogers).

When one examines the descriptions of how free association, inquiry, or "relationship" are implemented, one finds these conceptual labels refer to fairly elaborate sets of procedures. Each is not an operation, but a whole set of interrelated events involving verbal instructions as to what responses the patient should and should not make—a variety of questions, comments summarizing what the patient has said, evaluative statements, and nonverbal responses such as bodily position, smiles, voice inflections, and attentiveness. Thus, speaking about technique in such general terms tends to obscure the heterogeneity of procedures actually used and reduces the precision with which therapeutic operations can be communicated to others (pp. 675–676).

Ford and Urban conclude regarding therapy technique:

Typically, discussion of technique by these theorists utilizes higher-order concepts, without clear specification of the therapist behavior involved. Rogers' proposal that the therapist should convey unconditional positive regard to the patient is an example. By this he seems to mean that the therapist should think certain kinds of thoughts, have affectionate feelings toward the patient, and that he should make only some kinds of verbal statements and gestures. This concept covers a great deal of territory.

We think more careful specification on the part of all systems as
to the kinds of responses which are included under such abstract
concepts would help improve therapy technique and facilitate
the verification of the effects of the various kinds of therapeutic
procedures" (p. 680).

In Chapter 2 Strupp echos these comments.

How about the *dependent variable* in psychotherapy
theory? Kiesler (1966) stated:

Just as much imprecision has been manifest regarding the dependent variable in psychotherapy research. Here the Patient
Uniformity Myth has dictated the search for the one patient
process dimension along which beneficial patient change occurs.
For analytic therapy, this dimension has resided somewhere
among such variables as insight (making the unconscious conscious), working through, reduction in anxiety and resistance,
etc. For Rogers, it is found somewhere among his seven strands
of process or Experiencing. For behavior therapy it seems to re-
side somewhere in the process of anxiety reduction and symptom
removal (p. 129).

Just what kind of specific patient change does the therapist want to effect?

What should Mr. X talk about? Of what importance are his
feelings and attitudes toward the therapist? Should Mr. X be encouraged to feel friendly toward the therapist or will it be necessary for Mr. X to feel angry in the presence of the therapist
as a necessary step toward recognizing hostile feelings toward
his mother? Should Mr. X engage in associative chaining to permit the emergence of certain desired thoughts and feelings?
Should he seek introspectively to reproduce the feelings and attitudes appropriate to earlier events? Does he have to abreact? Is
intellectual insight required as an intermediate stage before certain changes can be expected? (Ford & Urban, 1963, p. 91).

Kiesler (1966) continues:

. . . since therapy is a sequential treatment procedure, one's model needs to be concerned further with the *dimension of time*. Are the same aspects of the therapist operative in the same pattern over the entire therapy interaction? If so, this needs to be explicitly defined theoretically. If, on one hand (as seems more likely), one or more therapist variables are crucial at one phase of the interaction, and others are indicated at other periods, then it is necessary to specify these time interactions. Otherwise a researcher may be sampling at the inappropriate therapy period in his attempt to investigate specific theoretical dimensions. Further, the model would be less difficult if psychotherapy were an agreed-upon perfect technique effecting change regardless of type and patient. However, since it seems more likely that psychotherapy represents in practice heterogeneous therapist performance depending upon the kind of patient with whom he is dealing, then one's model must delineate differential levels or classes of independent variables which are correlated respectively with these patient individual differences (p. 129).

Ford and Urban (1963) make the same point:

Some rationale about the order in which changes should be attempted is both a conceptual and procedural necessity. Conceptually, the therapist cannot deal with all the patient's difficulties simultaneously. Therefore, he needs some way of deciding what to respond to immediately, what to ignore, and what to defer until later; that is, he must have some notion about the order in which to proceed. Procedurally, it seems likely that there are certain sequences in which change can be accomplished most efficiently. In some instances it seems likely that *b* cannot be changed before *a* is modified—for example, resistance must first be interpreted away. Much more theoretical and research attention needs to be given to this issue (p. 686).

This point can be made differently by saying that one

cannot operate under an outcome uniformity myth. As Ford and Urban point out:

The major problem . . . is a lack of specification of what should be evaluated. *Clear specification of the behaviors to be changed makes easier the development of more effective procedures of appraisal.* One error frequently apparent in the literature should be avoided. *Appraisal should be based only on the behaviors the therapist attempted to change, and these differ from patient to patient.* For example, evaluation studies which assume that all patients will become less dependent are doomed to insignificant results, since not all patients need to change their dependence patterns (p. 688) . . . It is evident that the therapist cannot focus his attention and technique on all behavior patterns simultaneously. He will have to deal with one and then another, but the question then becomes, *"In what order should these changes be sought?"* A therapist is aware of the problem of sequence when he begins to consider such questions as the following: "What shall I encourage Mr. X to talk about first? He has many conflicting reactions to his mother: feelings of hate, fear, and love, as well as sexual impulses. Which of these should be talked about first? Perhaps the hostility, since he is less aware of his hate feelings than of the others. I must anticipate that making them explicit will bring fear and guilt along with it, so I must be prepared to deal with them next." Is the "transference neurosis" a necessary antecedent to the "abreaction" of infantile responses toward parental figures? Must "negative attitudes toward the self" be expressed before attitudes of "self-acceptance" can fully develop? Here we are trying to illustrate that in addition to setting long-range goals for the interview series, the therapist must, and at least implicitly does, work toward intermediate goals (p. 95).

Finally, none of the systems specify clearly what the *intra-therapy and extra-therapy changes* (and their interelations) should be. As Kiesler (1966) states:

Do we need different dependent variables of change for different kinds of patients? If so, what are the diagnostic dimensions involved, and what are the respective differential patient-change processes? Are these dependent variables manifest in the in-therapy verbal communications of the patient? If not, what are the extra-therapy manifestations of this change? If so, how are the in-therapy communication variables related to the extra-therapy manifestations? That is, how does the in-therapy process mediate changes in extra-therapy patient behaviors? It seems clear that the dependent variables of therapy are to be found somewhere in the in- or extra-therapy verbalizations and/or behavior of the patient, and in changes along these dimensions in a 'positive' direction over the therapy sequence (p. 129).

Ford and Urban (1963) comment on the same point:

As a group, these theorists devoted almost no systematic discussion to this issue. Most of them seemed to assume that changes accomplished in therapy would automatically generalize to other situations. Such a position would seem to be a logical outgrowth of the assumption that all behavior is controlled by habits of attention and thought; if one were to change these in therapy, and if the changed habits of attention and thought occurred in other situations as well, they might influence behavior in other situations. Of course, one wonders if the changes in the responses of attention and thought developed within therapy automatically transfer to other situations. We suspect they are far more likely to do so if special techniques are used to facilitate it. Some of the theorists spoke of discussing with the patient his attempts to change outside of therapy, but rarely did they specify any procedures . . . . This is a most important aspect of therapy and deserves far more systematic attention than it has received so far (p. 685–686).

Recapitulation

It seems apparent from this discussion that current theories of psychotherapy leave much to be desired. However, "behavior therapy" researchers more than other workers seem to be moving in the directions advocated in this and the next section. Wolpe, for example, does not talk about "the patient," but focuses on the phobic patient, and very specific techniques (desensitization) for changing very specific patient behaviors (fear reduction).

Kiesler (1966) and Breger and McGaugh (1965, 1966) have argued elsewhere that "behavior therapy" sometimes also falls into the uniformity myths described in this section, and sometimes underplays the subtle complexities involved in the application of their therapeutic treatments. For example, Wolpe states rather cavalierly in Chapter 1: "In some cases, such as most of the classical phobias in their usual forms, desensitization may be a straightforward matter. In other cases considerable skill is required of the therapist." Obviously, then, desensitization is not homogeneous and unidimensional. It would be interesting, at least, to know what are the parameters of "other cases" and "considerable skill."

Also, it seems the claims of Stampfl's implosive therapy are gradually widening so that it might be the treatment of choice for all types of patient disorder: "The method appears to be highly effective over a wide range of neurotic disorders including obsessive-compulsive and depressive reactions, and has been applied successfully to psychotic disorders including schizophrenic and depressive reactions. It shows promise in the treatment of characterological disorders including homosexuality, alcoholism, and stuttering" (Stampfl, 1967, p. 14). That about covers the scene! If it is that good, implosive therapy is tremendous and is *the* answer to psychopathology; but that probability seems quite small to this author. Stampfl's colleague, Levis (1967, p. 35), on the other hand, acknowledges that caution is necessary: ". . . it is prudent, at this point, to be cautious in the evaluation of Implosive

Therapy since it is historically well-known that 'new' therapies frequently appear to be more effective initially. The test of time will determine whether our present enthusiasm over the clinical and experimental data is warranted."

Ford and Urban (1967) articulate quite cogently some concerns about behavior therapy:

Adherence to a particular point of view can have real utility. It may focus effort and provide a framework within which to interpret findings. However, it can also lead to dogmatism, selective attention, ignorance, and derogation of the work of others. How to maintain its virtues without becoming prey to its liabilities is an old problem in the field of psychotherapy. Signs that the first is shading into the second begin to appear when it is said that no therapy is effective other than one's own, when what has been learned in the past is ignored in the enthusiasm of the present, when a view retains its internal coherence by ignoring external contributions, when new techniques are announced unrecognized as old ones described in new language, when major differences are obscured because a heterogeneity of approaches are referred to with one descriptive label, and when a special jargon is developed. This happened with psychoanalysis, some signs of it have appeared among some client-centered proponents, and some of it is beginning to occur in the newest movement called behavior therapy.

The many positive characteristics of this new emphasis will be discussed later. At this point, we would like to encourage the proponents not to institutionalize it into a "school." It seems to us inappropriate and inaccurate to do so. The term behavior therapy does not refer to a homogeneous group. Current approaches stem from a variety of rationales and employ differing techniques. The term itself is somewhat misleading. It developed originally to emphasize a focus on objectively observable aspects of behavior, but many in this movement are working with events which are "covert" and implicit, such as imagistic behavior. For some it implies changing behavior without involving awareness or thought but, for others in this general stream, those very responses are crucial. . . .

In seeking to derive procedures from experimental literature, this stream of development is not new. Many of the techniques are not new. What is new is the emphasis placed upon the systematic and detailed analysis of the presenting problem, concrete specification of the objectives to be obtained, selection of procedures (derived frequently from basic literature) in terms of the nature of the problem, orderly and systematic operations to implement the objectives, and some efforts to obtain an objective verification of the extent to which goals have been achieved (pp. 338, 339).

It seems that implosive therapy, as presented by Stampfl and Levis in *this* volume (Chapter 4), is most cautious about its claims of success. Its perceptive attempts to utilize psychoanalytic developmental constructs for hypotheses about the imagistic conditioned stimuli presented to the patient are unique for behavior therapy. Also, its attempt to explicate some of the complexities both in the sequence of cues, and the different content of these cues, to be presented to different types of patients is commendable.

Generally, it must be said that behavior therapy is an envigorating and promising challenge and contribution to the field of psychotherapy research. Primarily it represents a movement toward much greater specificity of therapist technique and patient change variables.

It is this author's contention that the same kind of theoretical and procedural specificity would be extremely useful for psychoanalytically-oriented psychotherapy.

A GRID MODEL
FOR THE PSYCHOTHERAPIES

It is easy to criticize existing systems without suggesting constructive alternatives. It is the purpose of this section to suggest strongly that alternative theories to those currently in vogue are at hand; the components of some have already been explicitly stated in various places; but unless these theoretical statements are systematically explicated, conforming to a paradigm similar to the one presented here, their impact and heuristic value will continue to be minimal.

Relatively few clinicians on the current psychotherapy scene adhere strictly to Freudian, existential, or behavior therapy regimes. Most describe themselves as eclectic, which implies that they extract "pieces" from each of the systems, modify them in accordance with their own experiences, and innovate as need arises. It is my contention that this eclectic lore, comprising the insights of clinicians who have been forced to modify traditional systems in dealing with different types of patients, offers the best promise for usefufl theoretical statements. Unfortunately, much of this lore is inexplicit and has not been recorded or communicated systematically. But this is the way it is usually stated: "Clinician A has a real feeling for working with paranoid schizophrenics and knows for example that if he is warm toward paranoids he'll drive them away. Clinician B has specialized in obsessive-compulsives and knows that reflection plays right into their ruminative defenses. Therefore he systematically challenges their contradictory statements. Clinician C communicates well with sociopaths and feels it is very important initially to outmanipulate and outshout his patients."

Obviously, if these clinical hunches are correct, then some very different therapist behaviors are occurring as a re-

sult of the type of patient, and the personality of the therapist. The problem with the hunches are that they comprise
loosely defined, inexplicit systems. Further, it is not very
clear what one means by "obsessive-compulsive," "paranoid
schizophrenic," or "sociopath"; interclinician reliability in assigning these labels to particular patients is rather low. Yet
these are not insurmountable problems, particularly if some
imaginative and articulate theoreticians arrive on the scene.

What is sorely needed, therefore, is not *a* theory of psychotherapy, but quite a few theories of psychotherapy—
theories respectively for obsessive-compulsives, hysterics,
anxiety reactions, phobics, process undifferentiated schizophrenics, depressive reactions, sociopaths and the like. Strupp
applies the same emphasis in Chapter 2 when he talks of systematic studies which will serve to restrict specific therapeutic
techniques to specific patients. The important point is that
these new formulations need to be stated explicitly and specifically enough so that the objections summarized in the
previous section do not apply.

Figure 1 presents schematically a model for the various
psychotherapies that avoids the inadequacies of present theories—the patient, therapist, and outcome uniformity assumptions. The multidimensions of therapist activity are specified
explicitly as are the in-therapy and concurrent or subsequent
extra-therapy changes on patient behavior that should occur.

The examples of patient types chosen and the specific
therapist and patient behaviors shown reflect to a degree the
author's thinking about these types of patients. But the specific variables presented are unimportant for the present purpose. The crucial aspect of the model is that it demonstrates
the kind of theoretical specificity that is necessary if we are
to make progress with the psychotherapies.

Notice the three surfaces of the model described in the

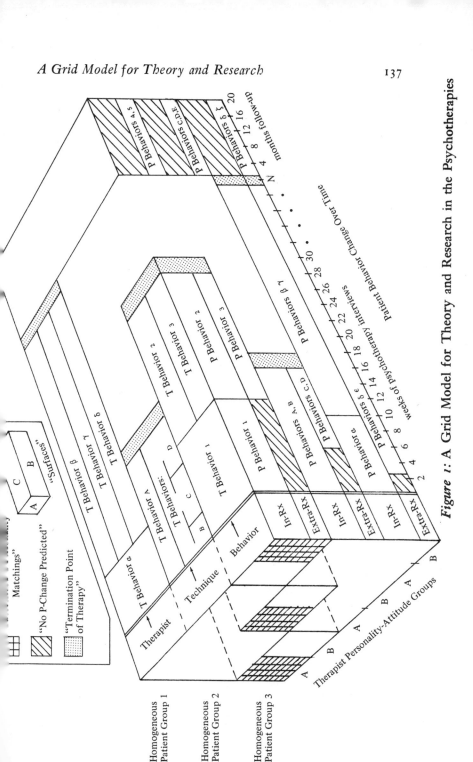

Figure 1: A Grid Model for Theory and Research in the Psychotherapies

legend. *Surface A* reflects the different types of patients for which separate theoretical statements are needed. The illustrative types chosen here—obsessive-compulsives, hysterics, mixed depressive-manics, and process undifferentiated schizophrenics—are arbitrarily chosen. In this regard, Wolpe as well as Stampfl and Levis should be commended for their focus on a restricted type of patient, the phobic. This kind of restriction of patient type, which avoids the patient uniformity myth, is needed in all theorizing about behavior modification. You will notice further on Surface A descriptions of what is meant by the various patient types, descriptions referring to the patient's manner of defensive communication or talking about himself. This emphasis derives from the author's attempts to operationalize one dimension of patient's talking-about-themselves behavior in the interview (Kiesler, Mathieu & Klein, 1964; Kiesler, Kline & Mathieu, 1965; Kiesler, Mathieu & Klein, 1967; Rogers, Gendlin, Kiesler, & Truax, 1967). Also it emphasizes the belief that researchers have ignored to a great extent the possibility that a patient's language behavior provides a good basis for eventual reliable and relevant psychiatric classification. As Kiesler states (1966):

A suggested answer to both of these nosological difficulties is that we may be looking in the wrong places for a reliable and valid diagnostic scheme. Perhaps the answer to the classification problem lies in differential patient behavior found in the therapy hour itself. If therapists in fact deal differently in therapy with different patients, then perhaps the patient cues to which the therapist differentially responds can be isolated and reliably measured from the interaction. If the manner in which the patient talks about himself in therapy indeed provides a reliable differentiation of patients, then the likelihood seems good that the process dimensions isolated would be directly relevant to differential therapeutic techniques. It seems that this possibility has been overlooked to date (p. 127).

Strupp argues in Chapter 2: the investigator of psychotherapy must abstract and quantify relevant aspects of the verbal interchange. Ruesch (1961) makes a similar point:

. . . only when we learn to diagnose the difficulties of our patients in terms of the same scientific universe in which we explain our therapeutic methods will we be able to evaluate therapy in a meaningful way. As long as the diagnosis is made in terms of one system and therapy is explained in terms of another system we cannot match therapy to pathology. Therefore it seems feasible that patients be diagnosed in terms of their ability to communicate and the disturbances that interfere with it. The therapeutic diagnosis thus is principally based upon the evaluation of the communicative behavior of the patient, and therapeutic communication is designed to overcome the difficulties (p. 74).

Turn now to *Surface B* in Figure 1. This represents a specification of the kind of changes that should occur in the respective types of patients. (1) Notice immediately that we are now not talking about "therapeutic outcome"; but rather about obsessive-compulsive outcome, hysteroid outcome, depressive-manic outcome, etc. This depicts clearly that we need different dimensions of change for different types of patients. Hence, we are avoiding here the outcome uniformity myth. (2) A clear distinction is made between two areas of patient change—that evident in the interview behavior of the patient (in-therapy change), and that apparent in the patient's behavior outside of therapy (with his peers, family, on the job, etc.), which is extra-therapy change. (3) Although it is not explicitly depicted in Figure 1, one should offer a specific rationale as to how, or whether, the in-therapy patient changes relate to the postulated extra-therapy changes. (4) It should also be evident that patient change is a multidimensional construct for a particular type of patient. Several different in- and extra-therapy behaviors should show change. (5) Further, the time dimension is specified, as well as the interaction of time with the specific patient changes. Some patient changes occur early in the therapy sequence, others will manifest themselves later, and still others cannot be expected until some time after therapy terminates. This aspect of the model emphasizes the necessity for repeated measures of patient changes (rather than the naive pre-post measurement of most "outcome" studies) along the several dimensions, and the important requirement of extended follow-up measurement for some patient-change behaviors. (6) The important variables of dosage and duration of therapy contact are also included. This implies that for some patients the changes expected should be accomplished over a four-month period; while for others two or more years of contact will be necessary. Some patients may require brief contacts daily, others may get by with an hour a week, and still others may need an hour daily for several weeks, and then little contact until the next crisis. Therapy dosage and duration of contact need to be theoretically specified.

Patient change obviously represents a complex construct, and needs to be specified in this kind of detail theoretically before we can usefully begin to research the "outcome" of "psychotherapy." This kind of theoretical specificity will aid researchers in making the operational and sampling decisions necessary to assess the predicted patient changes over the therapy sequence and subsequent follow-up periods.

Turn now to *Surface C* of Figure 1. This represents the related factors of therapist intervention that theoretically produce the specific patient changes for the respective types of patients. The surface avoids the therapist uniformity myth by attempting to specify the different therapist behaviors necessary to produce differential change with different types of patients.

Three general aspects of therapist behavior have been

emphasized by theory and research: (1) therapist "personality differences, exemplified by the research endeavors of Whitehorn & Betz (Betz, 1962); (2) therapist relationship-attitudes (e.g., positive regard, and congruence) emphasized by Rogers and the existentialists; and (3) therapist technique behavior—specific verbal and/or nonverbal manipulations by the therapist (e.g., "confrontation" or "interpretation").

It may be that therapist personality type needs to be matched in some way with patient type, as the figure suggests (*cf.* the "success" cells). It may further be the case that the attitudinal "conditions" emphasized by Rogers are important with every type of patient, however, although they may be necessary they are *in*sufficient conditions for effective patient changes. Finally, it seems very likely that if personality and attitudinal therapist factors are appropriate, it still remains that technique manipulations are extremely important and will vary with type of patient. Strupp in Chapter 2 also emphasizes the need for research in therapist skill as well as attitude and personality. Importantly, theoretical formulations must explicitly tie together these various aspects of the therapist's behavior, and specify the differences in behavior for the various types of patients.

As the model suggests, therapist behavior is very likely multi-dimensional and sequential. And inasmuch as changes desired in the patient are multidimensional, with different changes at different periods of time in the interactional sequence, the therapist model needs to specify individual therapist behaviors and their points of operation over time which correspond with respective changes in the patient. For example, after an initial period of communicated regard and empathy, "confrontation of contradictions" may be needed for a certain type of patient if his abstract talking is to be made more concrete.

Some Implications of the Model

It seems this kind of model, if correct, has important implications for research, training, and clinical practice. It argues for much more restricted and specific designs in research. For example, a group of homogeneous obsessive-compulsives, operationally defined (and here theoretical formulation would be a boon), could be assigned to therapists varying both in personality type and technical behavior. The latter behavior could be operationally prescribed to therapists in line with theoretical speculation. The sequence of techniques to modify respective patient behaviors could also be indicated. This would permit conclusions regarding the interaction of therapist personality, technique, and patient type (e.g., Technique B with therapist Personality C works best with obsessive-compulsives and thereby becomes the therapist-treatment of choice).

Similarly, in training therapists, we may first classify students regarding relevant personality dimensions. Assuming next that we have demonstrated the knowledge that would fill in the model in Figure 1, we say to a particular student, "It is very unlikely with your personality type that you'll ever work effectively with psychopathic patients. Instead, it seems likely you will do very well with obsessive-compulsives and with paranoid schizophrenics. Further, we know that a relatively rational approach of "confrontation of contradictions" and focus on patient role-playing behavior outside the interview are the treatments of choice for these patient types. Hence, we will focus our supervisory efforts primarily with these types of patients. We're going to make you an effective specialist—an expert in interpersonal relationships for obsessive-compulsive patients and paranoid schizophrenic patients. You'll not be all things to all patients, but you will be one hell of a specialist as we have described."

Finally, in clinics and private practice more time will be spent in the selection of patients, and we'll have a variety of psychotherapy specialists on the staff. The diagnostic and placement staffing might sound something like the following: "Patient X is obviously a hysteroid personality. Dr. B, you're a specialist with hysteroids—we've already established that your personality and techniques are the best for this type of patient. Hence, we are assigning Patient X to you. We certainly don't want to assign him to Dr. E, since we know that pairing has to be incompatible and the patient would terminate after three interviews."

In summary, then, the basic skeleton of a paradigm for psychotherapy seems to be something like the following: The patient communicates something; the therapist communicates something in response; the patient communicates and/or experiences something different; and the therapist, patient, and others like the change (although they may like it to different degrees, or for divergent reasons). What the therapist communicates (the independent variables) is very likely multidimensional (and the patterning of this multidimensionality needs to be specified), and may be different at different phases of the interaction for different kinds of patients. Similarly, what the patient communicates and/or experiences differently (the dependent variables) is likely multidimensional (and the patterning of that multidimensionality needs to be clarified) and may be different at distinct phases of the interaction. The enormous task of psychotherapy theory and research is that of filling in the variables of this paradigm (Kiesler, 1966, pp. 129–130).

It is hoped that the grid model presented here depicts this task more clearly and exemplifies some promising leads for the much needed theories of the psychotherapies.

REFERENCES

Betz, B. J. Experiences in research in psychotherapy with schizophrenic patients. In H. H. Strupp and L. Luborsky (Eds.), *Research in psychotherapy II*, Washington, D.C.: American Psychological Association, 1962. Pp. 41–60.

Breger, L., and McGaugh, J. L. Critique and reformulation of "learning-theory" aproaches to psychotherapy and neurosis. *Psychological Bulletin*, 1965, 63, 338–358.

Breger, L., and McGaugh, J. L. Learning theory and behavior therapy: A reply to Rachman and Eysenck. *Psychological Bulletin*, 1966, 65, 170–173.

Colby, K. M. Discussion of papers on therapist's contribution. In H. H. Strupp and L. Luborsky (Eds.), *Research in psychotherapy II*. Washington, D.C.: American Psychological Association, 1962. Pp. 95–101.

Colby, K. M. Psychotherapeutic processes. In *Annual Review of Psychology*, 1964, 15, 347–370.

Ford, D. H., and Urban, H. B. *Systems of psychotherapy*. New York: John Wiley & Sons, 1963.

Ford, D. H., and Urban, H. B. Psychotherapy. *Annual Review of Psychology*, 1967, 18, 333–372.

Kiesler, D. J. Some myths of psychotherapy research and the search for a paradigm. *Psychological Bulletin*, 1966, 65, 110–136.

Kiesler, D. J., Mathieu, P. L., and Klein, M. H. Sampling from the recorded therapy interview: A comparative study of different segment lengths. *Journal of Consulting Psychology*, 1964, 28, 349–357.

Kiesler, D. J., Klein, M. H., and Mathieu, P. L. Sampling from the recorded therapy interview: The problem of segment location. *Journal of Consulting Psychology*, 1965, 29, 337–344.

Kiesler, D. J., Mathieu, P. L., and Klein, M. H. Patient experiencing level and Interaction-Chronograph variables in therapy interview segments. *Journal of Consulting Psychology*, 1967, 31, 224.

Levis, D. J. Implosive therapy: the subhuman analogue, the strategy and the technique. In S. G. Armitage (Ed.), *Behavior modification techniques in the treatment of emotional disorders*, Battle Creek, Michigan: V.A. Publication, 1967. Pp. 22-37.

Phillips, E. L. *Psychotherapy: A modern theory and practice.* Englewood Cliffs, N. J.: Prentice-Hall, Inc., 1956.

Raimy, V. (Ed.), *Training in clinical psychology.* New York: Prentice-Hall, Inc., 1950.

Rogers, C. R., Gendlin, E. T., Kiesler, D. J., and Truax, C. B. *The therapeutic relationship and its impact: A study of psychotherapy with schizophrenics.* Madison, Wisconsin: University of Wisconsin Press, 1967.

Ruesch, J. *Therapeutic communication.* New York: W. W. Norton Co., 1961.

Stampfl, T. G. Implosive therapy: The theory. In S. G. Armitage (Ed.), *Behavior modification techniques in the treatment of emotional disorders.* Battle Creek, Michigan: V. A. Publication, 1967. Pp. 12-21.

6

OVERVIEW

LEONARD D. ERON and ROBERT CALLAHAN

THE THEME OF THIS volume constitutes a very important problem for practicing clinical psychologists. What is the relationship, if any, between the theoretical orientation of the therapist—his ideas about how personality develops and changes, as well as his notions about what should transpire in a therapeutic interaction—and what he actually does or attempts to achieve in a series of therapeutic encounters? As practitioners of an applied science, it would be well if we could claim that our procedures stem directly from a comprehensive body of theory and research. As pragmatic American psychologists, coming from a tradition of behaviorism and functionalism, we would like to demonstrate that our theory points directly to operations and it is through these operations that reconstruction and modification of personality and behavior are effected. The editors of this volume, on reviewing its contributions, are impressed with the fact that although we are slowly approaching this goal, we still have a long and tedious way to go.

Strupp and Stampfl and Levis concern themselves directly with the problem at hand; the other authors do so only indirectly. Strupp reports on a program of research attempting to define certain therapist parameters and to predict from these to therapeutic process and outcome. Sometimes the variables he deals with stem from a theory of interpersonal behavior, psychoanalysis; more often the therapist variables have been researched because they are obvious ones which can be counted and measured. Kiesler describes a more comprehensive superstructure of therapist and patient variables, but avoids defining underlying parameters for his dimensions. If all the cells in Kiesler's model were successfully filled with empirical data, we would then perhaps be able to construct a theory to account for all the predictions. But Kiesler does not proceed from a well-defined theory to delineate specific behaviors which are likely to bring about change in the patient. He is concerned about the problem of dimensionality but does not involve himself with the interaction among factors which Strupp strongly emphasizes in his work and presentation.

Strupp's summary of the relevant research indicates not only that therapist variables are important in determining what happens in psychotherapy but also that what the therapist does is related to his theoretical orientation, despite the fact that many therapists, especially the more experienced ones, do much the same thing regardless of theoretical orientation. However, he does not consider the possibility that those differences that do emerge are a function not of specific theories and the operations to which they lead but rather of the personality of the practitioners who choose one theory over another.

Stampfl and Levis state a theoretical position based primarily on animal studies, and they demonstrate how the behavior of the therapist derives directly from the theory that psychopathological behavior represents avoidance of conditioned anxiety. Although this attempt is probably the most appropriate contribution in terms of the theme of this volume, they have not presented data to support the validity of what they are attempting to do. Indeed, their techniques of therapeutic interaction derive from a theory, but the studies they cite are laboratory studies with lower animals. It remains to be demonstrated that these techniques are effective therapeutically. We would be hard put to demonstrate that lower animals engage in fantasy and the other forms of symbolic behavior which constitute the core of what goes on in the Stampfl-Levis form of behavior therapy.

Stampfl and Levis give examples of four kinds of symptom complexes to which their recommended procedures can be applied with success. Should we assume that implosive therapy is limited to these? They themselves, in their concluding statement, caution that the effectiveness of their approach has yet to be determined empirically. If carefully controlled studies of "in vivo" therapy eventually support their position, we will indeed have a therapy in which the maneuvers of the therapist derive directly from a theory of behavior. However, Wolpe in his chapter takes a very pessimistic view of the likelihood of achieving positive results with a behavior theory based on the phenomenon of extinction.

Parenthetically, it should be noted here that studies dealing with the outcome of psychotherapy are highly unsatisfactory in design and credibility. As yet, there have not been devised any consistent, reliable measures of therapeutic success, and whatever data are available can be interpreted to support all views. Analogue studies which deal with the process of psychotherapy suffer from the weakness of the analogue argument—they are not really analogous to psychotherapy. Consequently, they do not illuminate the outcome problem nor do they help define the process of psychotherapy. They are interesting and unique, but stand by themselves.

This is related to another problem in evaluating results of behavior therapy. The behavior therapists in this volume list symptom complexes for which they feel their techniques are specific, but it is important to point out that these are not the problems with which most therapists usually deal. Phobias are rare and relatively accessible to modifications by many simple techniques, including drugs. Most behavior disorders with which therapists are faced are not symptom-specific but usually are composed of diffuse psychological disturbances and marked situational difficulties, a point cogently made by Strupp.

Equally unrealistic are the psychoanalytic therapists who, as Strupp also points out, require extensive and stringent criteria for acceptance as a good psychotherapy risk. If this is so, the theory effectively rules out any test of itself in practice due to the scarcity of such paragons. In this regard, behavior therapy theory is more appealing since it is democratic and does not restrict its efforts to a small elite.

A refreshing aspect of the Stampfl-Levis behavior theory approach is that it does not regard practitioners of other theoretical persuasions as fools or charlatans. In fact, they refer primarily to dynamic or psychoanalytic formulations in deriving hypotheses about the traumatic events the patient is trying to avoid by way of his psychopathology. The method which Wolpe recommends, however, is a "know nothing" approach in which the therapist puts on blinders, disregarding much of what has been learned about personality and behavior over the last seventy-five years. In this regard, this latter-day Pavlovian resembles those psychopathologists who insist that all attempts at classification are useless (See Volume 1 of this series, Eron, 1966). By disregarding knowledge and experience that has accrued from earlier attempts at classification and theory construction, he is closing his eyes to potentially important behavioral phenomena that may be relevant to the practice of psychotherapy and behavioral change.

While the behavior therapist may be accused of contriving artificial situations, Rosenbaum is intimately concerned with the real "problems in living." In this symposium, however, he addresses himself only indirectly to the problem of technique and theory relationships and primarily emphasizes the ethics of the therapeutic relationship. Although this is interesting and important, it does not appear to be directly influential in the development of technique. Strupp attacks this position very directly with his comments on the irrelevance of the existentialist position as to what goes on in therapy and the complete lack of concern with outcome. As Strupp sees it, existential therapists do not use any different techniques than psychoanalysts and with this Rosenbaum agrees. However, Rosenbaum seems overly concerned with the value system that is attached to the therapeutic process without giving any evidence of the influence, if any, of the value system upon the technique of therapy. In other writings of Rosenbaum (Mullan and Rosenbaum, 1962; Rosenbaum, 1965) technique has been emphasized and it is interesting that he is now turning to these philosophical considerations. It seems as though he is agreeing with Strupp that, as yet, the therapist variables that have been investigated are relatively unimportant. But Strupp continues to pursue a course of manipulating these variables while Rosenbaum is content to retire to the armchair. Again his philosophical concerns are interesting but not relevant to the problem at hand.

In considering Rosenbaum's philosophical discussion, it should be pointed out that he is not clear about the relationship between logical positivism and experiential psychology. Although he identifies Freud as a logical positivist, we are quite sure he will not find many philosophers of science who would agree with him. He compounds the confusion by differentiating psychoanalysis from existentialism on the grounds that the former is operational and the latter mystical.

Rosenbaum and the behavior therapists refer to the therapist as an expert, although Rosenbaum objects and insists that the relationship with the patient should be one between peers. This approach leads to the strong emphasis by Rosenbaum upon the interaction between therapist and patient, in contrast to the complete lack of any consideration on this interaction by the behavior therapists. Here we are more sympathetic to Rosenbaum's emphasis. It might be hypothesized that the behavior changes occurring in behavior therapy are a direct result of transference phenomena, although as yet no adequate tests of this position have been made. Those studies that use variants of treatment approaches which purport to show the superiority of behavior over depth therapy are inappropriate, since they are usually based upon analogues and nonpathological behavior (e.g. Paul, 1966).

Rosenbaum's insistence upon the consideration of ethics in therapy does not delineate techniques of changing pathological behavior. Regardless of ethical questions, the underlying principle followed by therapists is that pathological behavior should be changed. The crux of the problem is the pathological nature of the behavior and not the value system of the therapist or the patient. A disturbance in the value system or ethics of an individual does not lead to pathological thinking, and for the therapist to understand pathological thinking, he does not himself have to engage in it.

An incidental comment on Rosenbaum's presentation is that it is gratuitous to invoke unresolved relationships with parents as explanations for theoretical positions taken by writers and researchers (e.g., Rosenbaum's reference to Jones). Using this approach it could probably be shown that Leibnitz derived the calculus due to an unresolved relationship with his mother and father. But what does this add to our knowledge of differential equations?

Kiesler, in constructing his "paradigm," clearly does a service in pointing out the large gaps in our current knowledge of the variables of psychotherapy and their importance. However, he does little to clarify the relationship between theory and technique as posed for this volume. In fact, it seems to us that he unnecessarily compounds the complexity by using important variables without any reference to theory. He has followed Kraepelin without the careful clinical observation that typifies Kraepelin's classification system. Consequently, he has formulated a descriptive system that has organizational appeal but upon careful perusal leads to some confusion. His descriptive system is less than inclusive and his dimensions are poorly defined; e.g., it is not clear how time can be a dimension when it is a direct result of the interaction between the dimensions of disorder and type of treatment. All of this leads to an exercise in collecting small nuggets of information without any overall direction that should come from an understanding of the determinants of behavior and behavior change. It is difficult to differentiate the dependent and independent variables in his "paradigm" and to determine their dimensional units. To illustrate this criticism, the reader should attempt to formulate experiments that derive directly from Kiesler's "paradigm" and this point will become apparent. Although Kiesler sees many commonalities between his approach and that of Stampfl and Levis, he does not consider the very sharp differences. Stampfl and Levis consistently proceed from theoretical formulations in explicating their technique while Kiesler takes an inductive approach and attempts to formulate techniques from disparate sources, including unique experiences with patients. Kiesler is very concrete in building his "paradigm" as exemplified by his use of diagnostic labels, specific behaviors, limited time units and specific therapist characteristics. Although he is obviously aware of the artificiality of our current classification systems, he does not find it possible to avoid using them. Actually Kiesler leans more toward what he defines as the unique approach than do any of the other writers in this volume. He meticulously categorizes types of therapists, selects specific diagnostic categories, uses very discrete therapeutic responses, and divides time into extra and intra therapeutic contact. Since there is no underlying commonality on which to compare all of these dimensions, his pictorial representation (Figure 1) implies an interactive relationship that has not been defined and a continuity between his categories that is not apparent.

Further, there is a real problem in applying Kiesler's approach to practice. Although it would be nice to be able to prescribe a specialized therapist, expert in a specific procedure, for a "unique" patient, it is impossible to foresee that there will ever be sufficient therapists to satisfy all Kiesler's conditions.

There is a fundamental difference between the two behavior therapy positions developed in this volume. Although they both profess to base their practice upon classical conditioning, Wolpe is diametrically opposed to Stampfl and Levis in his use of this theoretical orientation. Wolpe insists that the basic therapeutic mechanism is the pairing of a strong, nonanxious response with a weak anxiety response elicited by the anxiety-producing stimulus, while Stampfl and Levis stress that experimental extinction is the only effective agent in removing anxiety. Both report therapeutic successes using these techniques but neither of them has an explanation for the purported successes of the other. In fact, Wolpe minimizes the efficacy of Stampfl and Levis' system by appealing to his own experience in therapy and points out the lack of innovation in their approach.

The definition of anxiety presents another disparity between the two behavior therapists. Wolpe operationally defines anxiety as all inclusive and not different physiologically from fear. This is highly questionable (c.f. Mahl, 1952; and Funkenstein, 1957; Grinker, 1961) and appears to oversimplify the complexity of anxiety. Historically, the differentiation of anxiety from fear has been an important concept in understanding the basic mechanisms in neurosis (Freud, 1959). Stampfl and Levis accept the physiological differentiation between fear and anxiety and in addition make use of psychodynamic formulations in their technique.

While historically Wolpe has been closely bound in practice to his theoretical position, it can be readily seen that attempts have been made to expand the techniques to meet varied therapeutic problems; theory thus has become less consistent and dominated by technique evolving on a pragmatic basis. For example, he lists in his bag of tricks assertive therapy, sexual therapy, aversive conditioning, positive reconditioning, muscle relaxation, and finally reciprocal inhibition. One would suspect that the elegance and thoroughness of the development of implosive therapy will also succumb to this same insidious influence. Stampfl and Levis now cite four specific problems requiring special techniques and like Wolpe could easily arrive eventually at a grand smorgasbord.

In considering Wolpe's examples of representative behavior therapy cases, we specifically take exception to his sexual therapy. When he describes the treatment of sexual inadequacy in a male patient, he does not consider the effect of the rational-educational therapy given to the wife. We would consider this as more effective in reconstituting the husband's potency than the construction of a sexual anxiety hierarchy for the husband. Paradoxically, as the wife relaxes, she makes it harder for her husband. Secondly, we object to the inference that anxiety hierarchies are pathological. Obviously, anxiety hierarchies can be constructed for an adequately functioning individual. We would consider this a case of reality testing. Another minor but important point is that Wolpe does use the dynamic approach when he sees it as applicable. In his discussion of homosexuality, he clearly accepts the notion that the symptom is not the neurosis, for as he states, "many cases . . . are based on neurotic interpersonal anxiety; if this is removed, the homosexual behavior often disappears entirely."

The problem of symptom substitution is a favorite point of contention between the behavior therapists and the dynamic therapists. In our opinion, it is an artificial argument since there is no evidence in the dynamic position that symptom removal without reference to the underlying dynamics should inevitably lead to symptom substitution. The dynamic position is not invalidated because substitution does not occur. Very often, the removal of the symptom changes the dynamic organization of the personality and it may therefore not be necessary for another symptom to appear in place of the one that has been removed through treatment.

Stampfl and Levis tend to reduce the human condition to very simple levels. To equate the effect of a buzzer as a CS with the real-life experience of having a large, aggressive, highly voluble, and emotionally overwrought father bearing down upon the children with a shovel in his hand is highly suspect. Certainly this is recognized by Stampfl and Levis, but they are insistent upon using animal experimentation as evidence for the validity of their techniques.

It is less than clear as to how the emphasis upon the avoidant response reduces the original anxiety. For example, if the patient extinguishes his anxiety to aggressive acting out, what is to prevent him from acting out without anxiety? Would not this acting out then lead to new pain and a recurrence of anxiety? On the other hand, if depression permits the patient to avoid the anxiety-arousing implications of his aggressive desires, why encourage him to dwell on his feelings of worthlessness and inadequacy? It is not clearly spelled out how the exaggeration of the avoidant response eliminates it as a defense.

Also Stampfl and Levis ignore the problem of secondary gain. This is especially true when the patient is encouraged by a strong authority figure to fantasize every kind of tabooed subject without fear of condemnation. This may make therapy pleasurable and be the real impetus for maintaining the patient in therapy.

Finally, it is striking how Stampfl and Levis ignore the similarity of their procedure for inducing fantasy to other more established psychotherapeutic techniques, such as hypnotherapy, psychodrama, and even more basically the "working through" of the classical analyst.

In summarizing our feelings about these papers, we would like to point out their positive values. The behavior therapists are on the right track in their insistence upon theoretical justification for the actions of the therapist. Strupp, although making the same point, enhances the relationship between theory and practice by minimizing animal studies and concentrating on research involving humans in order to develop theoretical formulations. Kiesler and Rosenbaum discuss interesting components of the theme, in that Rosenbaum makes an important ethical point and Kiesler illuminates the complexity of the problem. For us, we find the Strupp paper most attractive, closely followed by the Stampfl and Levis paper as being the most substantial in demonstrating that what transpires in psychotherapy can derive directly from a theory of behavior. Wolpe restates the behavior therapy position based on classical conditioning but does not expand his previous position. Rosenbaum continually keeps us focused upon the humanistic considerations of therapeutic relationships which makes for a fitting conclusion to this volume.

REFERENCES

Eron L. D. (Ed.), *Classification of the behavior disorders*. Chicago: Aldine, 1966.

Freud, S. *Inhibition, symptoms and anxiety*, Standard Edition. London: Hogarth Press, 1959.

Funkenstein, D. H., King, S. H., and Drolette, M. E. *Mastery of stress*. Cambridge: Harvard University Press, 1957.

Grinker, R. R., Miller, J., Sabshin, M., Nunn, R., and Nunnally, J. C. *The phenomena of depression*. New York: Paul B. Hoeber, 1961.

Mahl, F. Relation between acute and chronic fear and the gastric audity and blood sugar levels in macaca mulatta monkeys. *Psychosomatic Medicine*, 1952, 14, 182–210.

Mullan, H., and Rosenbaum, M. *Group psychotherapy: theory and practice*. New York: Free Press, 1962.

Paul, G. L. *Insight vs. desensitization in psychotherapy, an experiment in anxiety reduction.* Stanford: Stanford University Press, 1966.

Rosenbaum, M. Group psychotherapy and psychodrama. Chapter 45 in B. B. Wolman (Ed.), *Handbook of clinical psychology.* New York: McGraw-Hill, 1965.

7

RESPONSES TO
THE OVERVIEW

ROBERT CALLAHAN and LEONARD D. ERON

UPON COMPLETION of the Overview by the editors, it was
circulated for the authors' comments. Joseph Wolpe, Max
Rosenbaum, and Thomas Stampfl and Donald Levis found
points in the Overview they thought not quite adequate in
reflecting their position. Neither Hans Strupp nor Donald
Kiesler felt it necessary to comment on the Overview, although this lack does not imply complete agreement with it.
Thus, the content of this chapter is a report of the comments
made about the Overview, starting with Joseph Wolpe's re-
statement of his strong behavioristic orientation and his support of behavior therapy. He feels that the editors have been
less than accepting of the behavior therapy literature and,
also, arbitrary in some of their differences.

JOSEPH WOLPE:

Quite a few misconceptions are revealed in this Overview, which I shall discuss in the order in which they appear.

(1) Eron and Callahan allege that the applications of behavior therapy are "limited" because "phobias are rare and relatively accessible to modification by many simple techniques including drugs." I have repeatedly pointed out that even if classical phobias are not particularly common, the vast majority of neuroses can be seen, on behavioral analysis, to be at bottom persistent unadaptive anxiety habits. Once the stimulus antecedents of the reactions that make up the habit have been identified, deconditioning can be effected, and such secondary manifestations as psychosomatic symptoms, sexual inadequacies, character disorders, and obsessional behavior *pari passu* diminished and disappear. I have seen many patients who, after prolonged but unsuccessful treatment by psychoanalysis for character neuroses, have re-complaint that "Wolpe recommends . . . a know nothing covered through the application of behavior therapy. The approach . . . disregarding much of what has been learned about personality and behavior over the last seventy-five years" really has very little substance to it. How much of this "knowledge" has any scientifically acceptable support, though it is generally treated as though it were fully established?

(2) They dismiss Paul's study on the altogether arbitrary ground that it is based upon "nonpathological behavior" in alleged contrast to what is encountered in the clinic. Paul's subjects were unadaptively disturbed in specified situations and had real disabilities. This seems to be the essence of more complicated cases also. If Eron and Callahan believe that one is "pathological" and the other not, the onus is upon them to

point to precisely what constitutes the difference. Paul's study actually contradicts in the most impressive way the supposition that the "changes occurring in behavior therapy are a direct result of transference phenomena."

In discussing the two "behavior therapy positions" discussed in this volume, a distinction must be made between the practices and their explanations. While I tend most often to use a gradual desensitizing type of technique, I also on occasion subject patients to highly anxiety-producing stimuli and there is no doubt that this sometimes works. What I do not agree with is the explanation provided by Stampfl and Levis, a matter that I have discussed elsewhere (Wolpe, 1968).

A desultory attitude to the behavior therapy literature is revealed repeatedly. It is stated that the correspondence between practice and theory has become less consistent. In fact, every one of the techniques—assertive therapy, sexual therapy, desensitization, positive reconditioning and others— has a clear-cut rationale in learning mechanisms (Wolpe, 1958). The same casualness is shown in the statement that in the treatment of sexual inadequacies in a male, the role of the wife as the basis of change is ignored. The wife's use as a collaborator does imply some change in her attitudes, but until the procedures are gone through *according to prescription*, change does not occur. Again, to object to the idea that anxiety hierarchies are pathological is to be oblivious of the fact that hierarchies are constructed only of material to which anxiety is unadaptive. A similar oblivion must lie behind the suggestion of a concession to the dynamic approach in the notion that homosexual behavior may disappear if neurotic interpersonal anxiety is removed. There is a simple behavioristic explanation—that if interpersonal fear is conditioned to females more than to males there will be a displacement of approach responses away from the female end of the spectrum; and after deconditioning of the fear the normal heterosexual preference may assert itself.

MAX ROSENBAUM:

I question the concept of American psychologists "coming from a tradition of behaviorism and functionalism." Underneath this concept is the theme of the physical sciences as the model for research in psychotherapy. I question whether the methods of the physical sciences are applicable to research in psychotherapy. I cannot stress this point strongly enough. Julian Huxley, the biologist, described this as "the finest theory defeated by the ugly fact." The mechanistic approach is fundamental to the behavioral therapists and their approach. As for Stampfl and Levis, whose studies I have followed, I find it hard to extrapolate animal research to human behavior.

I feel that technique often masks the philosophical problems involved. To illustrate: In a course on group therapy and family therapy the students discussed Ackerman's work and a particular case reported by him. In this case, the husband and wife are discussing their sex life and the wife's feeling about sex and the husband's use of a condom. It is not clear from the test as to whether the daughter Peg, eleven years old, remained in the room while this discussion was being carried on. One of the students brought up the question, "Why can't the child listen to this discussion? In my hospital setting, everything is discussed." Another student asked, "How does this help or hamper Peg?" Before long, there was a discussion as to whether it would be appropriate for the child to be witness to sexual intercourse between parents. After all, some of the students commented, Virginia Satir, the West Coast exponent of family therapy, has raised serious questions about the family structure in our society.

How long should a family be kept together as a unit, and isn't it time for modifications in the structure of the family? Doesn't the "rational" Albert Ellis concur with Satir? Isn't there an entire value system at work in this mechanical exposition of family therapy. I have been constantly concerned with the concept of privacy in psychotherapy. There is now a proliferation of video tapes, tape recordings (voice), and one-way screens. How do these affect the technique of psychotherapy. Where does the value system of confidentiality enter into this?

Concerning existentialism, there is one very basic point. Existentialism embraces many disparate viewpoints and there is no validity to the general statement that existentialists, who are indeed a large group of psychotherapists, are unconcerned with the outcome of therapy. There is always a concern for the value system—and specifically, following Martin Buber, a concern with the meaning of mutualism. Preoccupation with technique obscures a philosophy and a value system. Unless we explore philosophical concerns we become technicians wildly scrambling to new techniques as we become frantic about the last technique that didn't work.

Freud was a logical positivist and based his concepts on a biological framework. He followed Darwin's path and did not approve of Adler's concern with social needs and the structure of society. Adler would sit in a coffee house at night, meeting his patients there, carrying out his early versions of group therapy. Freud would not accept Adler's unkempt appearance, much less his socializing with patients. Freud stated that he could not bear his patients to look at him all day long, hence, he held on to the couch he first used when he practiced hypnosis. Adler was a political activist and his approach to life influenced his approach to his therapy.

Let us note this question of pathological behavior. In a

very good summary (Siegler and Osmond, 1966), there is a presentation of biochemical, genetic, psychoanalytic, interactional, and moral theories. These theories were sorted into six models: medical, moral, psychoanalytic, family interaction, conspiratorial, and social. For every model there was a philosophy and a value system to be found as quite basic. So what is pathology? If schizophrenia is truly genetic do we have the right to sterilize schizophrenics?

Now play fair about unresolved relationships with parents; all of Freud's inner circle reacted to him as Papa Freud. When Ruth Mack Brunswick analyzed again the case of the Russian nobleman (Freud's Wolfman), she was extremely hesitant to publish it since she had much material that Freud had missed. I don't know whether Leibnitz derived calculus because of his problems with his parents, but I cite his writings on theology and his effort to reconcile the Protestant and Catholic faiths. There have been many recorded incidents of great figures in science who were stimulated in their work by deep and unresolved problems.

Incidentally, many analysts claim that anxiety is what moves people to change—so what does Wolpe's position really mean?

THOMAS STAMPFL and DONALD LEVIS:

In the interest of clarification, we would like to comment briefly on the following twelve statements made by Eron and Callahan in Chapter 6. Their statement will be quoted first followed by our commentary.

Indeed their techniques of therapeutic interaction derive from a theory but the studies they cite are laboratory studies with lower animals. It remains to be demonstrated that these techniques are effective therapeutically.

Perhaps we are unclear on this point. Our concluding paragraph refers to studies of therapeutic effectiveness on the human level which made use of control groups and objective criteria of improvement (Hogan, 1966; Kirchner & Hogan, 1966; Hogan & Kirchner, 1967; Levis & Carrera, 1967; Barrett, 1968). These studies support the therapeutic effectiveness of IT techniques. Of course, much remains to be done in outcome research. The animal experiments are not intended to validate the techniques employed with human subjects but rather are designed to test in a laboratory setting theoretical *principles* upon which the techniques are derived. The validation of the technique is a separate question.

We would be hard put to demonstrate that lower animals engage in fantasy and the other forms of symbolic behavior which constitutes the core of what goes on in the Stampfl-Levis form of behavior therapy.

One need not demonstrate that animals fantasize, but only that *in principle* fantasy and other internally elicited cues in the human are capable of analysis of S-R terms in the same way that an S-R model can be applied to lower animals. Thus, the cues on the human level function as conditioned aversive stimuli which develop and maintain symptomatology.

Stampfl and Levis give examples of four kinds of symptom complexes to which their recommended procedures can be applied with success. Should we assume that implosive therapy is limited to these?

We intended to present a "learning analysis of the etiology of a few *sample* symptoms," (italics added) in order to illustrate the use of hypothesized conditioned aversive cues. Limitations of space precluded an exhaustive treatment of the gamut of psychopathological reactions and the wide variety of associated cues (see Stampfl and Levis, 1967 a, b).

If carefully controlled studies of "in vivo" therapy eventually support their position, we will indeed have a therapy in which the maneuvers of the therapist derive directly from a theory of behavior. However, Wolpe, in his chapter, takes a very pessimistic view of the likelihood of achieving positive results with a behavior theory based on the phenomenon of extinction.

We regard this problem as an essentially empirical matter. Of course, Wolpe is entitled to his opinion. The available evidence tends to support the *empirical* law of extinction (nonreinforcement) on both the human and infrahuman level (Wolpin & Pearsall, 1965; Nelson, 1966; Wolpin and Raines, 1966; Myerhoff, 1967; Barrett, 1968).

. . . while Stampfl and Levis stress that experimental extinction is the only effective agent in removing anxiety.

Empirically, there have been at least two procedures considered to be effective in eliminating conditioned responses—nonreinforcement and counterconditioning. We have selected one of these operations, that of nonreinforcement, but this *does not*, of course, imply a rejection of the empirical principle of counterconditioning. On the theoretical level the problem is more complicated, and at the time of this writing we have not taken a strong position on the matter.

Stampfl and Levis . . . like Wolpe could easily arrive eventually at a grand smorgasbord.

Adherence to the principles of aversive conditioning is at stake here. Quite a variety of techniques might follow the same principle. Certainly, one must be careful of circularity in applying these principles to the human situation. On the other hand, it is evident that a wide range of cues is conditionable. Multiplicity of cues should not be taken as an indication of a "smorgasbord" of techniques if the nonreinforcement principle is consistently followed.

Another minor but important point is that Wolpe does use the dynamic approach when he sees it as applicable.

This point is extremely well taken. Wolpe denies it, but it seems obvious.

Stampfl and Levis tend to reduce the human condition to very simple levels. To equate the effect of a buzzer as a CS with the real life experience . . . is highly suspect.

Our main point in our paper was that such a real life situation as described *is not* comparable to the typical animal conditioning paradigm where a single CS such as a buzzer is used. A more adequate animal analogue would involve multiple stimulus elements such as buzzer, tone, lights, door up, and floor withdrawal arranged in a sequential order (Stampfl, 1961; Levis, 1966).

. . . if the patient extinguishes his anxiety to aggressive acting out, what is to prevent him from acting out without anxiety?

We argue that aggressive acting out is based on the emotional response of anger conditioned to stimuli correlated with experiences of frustration. The reinforcement for the anger response which motivates aggressive behavior is the *consequence* of the frustration experience, such as organic deprivation. Anger, like anxiety, is extinguishable in terms of the principle of nonreinforcement. Thus, anger responses are elicited to frustration stimuli in the absence of the consequences of frustration. Since anger as the secondary drive state which furnishes the motivation for aggressive responses is reduced, the tendency to engage in aggressive acting out responses is also reduced.

On the other hand, if depression permits the patient to avoid the anxiety-arousing implications of his aggressive desires, why encourage him to dwell on his feelings of worthlessness and inadequacy. It is not clearly spelled out how the exaggeration of the avoidant response eliminates it as a defense.

Depression represents a relative failure of avoidance, but the failure is not complete. We strive to make it complete in order to obtain a maximal extinction effect to the full range of cues eliciting the emotional response labeled depression. We do not try to exaggerate the avoidant response, but strive to introduce those cues which would be coincident with the failure of avoidance.

Also Stampfl and Levis ignore the problem of secondary gain.

This would be difficult to test on the human level, and indicates the need to conduct *some* experimentation on the animal level as a check on the general validity of the model.

Finally, it is striking how Stampfl and Levis ignore the similarity of their procedures for inducing fantasy to other more established psychotherapeutic techniques . . .

We agree that there are similarities to other psychotherapeutic procedures such as those cited. These have been touched on elsewhere. Unfortunately, an adequate analysis of the similarity of IT to other techniques would be lengthy —limitations of space precluded such an analysis. However, adherence to an avoidance learning model leads to some rather profound dissimilarities both on the level of technique and theory. We plan to deal with these at length in future publications.

In conclusion, these comments by the contributors illustrate that there are sharp differences still remaining in the conceptualization of therapy, the approaches to the treating of pathology, the experimental procedures most fruitful in investigating these conceptual differences, and even more clearly the techniques most efficacious in achieving therapeutic improvement. It is felt that the comments by Joseph Wolpe are well taken but essentially restate his points as given in his original contribution and do not directly meet the objections raised by the chapter. Certainly, there is no easy answer to these objections except, as Stampfl and Levis point out, empirical evidence would be extremely helpful. The Stampfl and Levis comments are specific and to the point and tend to again emphasize their strong reliance upon animal experimentation to support their theoretical orientation. In conclusion, Max Rosenbaum maintains his strong humanistic approach and tends to see behavior therapy as contrary to the welfare of humanity.

REFERENCES

Barrett, C. L. Systematic desensitization therapy (SDT) versus implosive therapy (IT): A comparative study of the efficiency of two behavior therapies in reducing snake phobic behavior in otherwise normal adults. *Unpublished dissertation,* University of Louisville, 1968.

Hogan, R. A. Implosive therapy in the short term treatment of psychotics. *Psychotherapy: Theory, Research and Practice,* 1966, *3,* 25–32.

Hogan, R. A., and Kirchner, J. H. Preliminary report of the extinction of learned fears via short-term implosive therapy. *Journal of Abnormal Psychology,* 1967, *72,* 106–109.

Kirchner, J. H., and Hogan, R. A. The therapist variable in the implosion of phobias. *Psychotherapy: Theory, Research and Practice,* 1966, *3,* 102–104.

Levis, D. J. Effects of serial CS presentation and other characteristics of the CS on the conditioned avoidance response. *Psychological Reports,* 1966, *18,* 755–766.

Levis, D. J., and Carrera, R. N. Effects of ten hours of implosive therapy in the treatment of outpatients. *Journal of Abnormal Psychology*, 1967, 72, 504–508.

Myerhoff, H. L. Tension and anxiety in deconditioning. *Unpublished dissertation*, University of Southern California, 1967.

Nelson, F. Effects of two counterconditioning procedures on the extinction of fear. *Journal of Comparative and Physiological Psychology*, 1966, *62*, 208–213.

Siegler, M., and Osmond, H. Models of madness. *British Journal of Psychiatry*, 1966, *112*, 1193–1203.

Stampfl, T. G. Acquisition and resistance to extinction of avoidance responses to simple, congruent, and serial-congruent conditioned stimuli. *Unpublished manuscript*, 1962.

Stampfl, T. G., and Levis, D. J. Essentials of implosive therapy: A learning-based psychodynamic behavioral theory. *Journal of Abnormal Psychology*, 1967, 72, 496–503.

Stampfl, T. G., and Levis, D. J. Implosive therapy. In R. M. Jurjevich (Ed.), *Handbook of direct and behavior psychotherapies*. Englewood Cliffs, N.J.: Prentice-Hall, 1968.

Wolpe, J. Principles and techniques for eliminating unadaptive emotional reactions. In D. S. Jacobs (Ed.), *The behavior therapies*. (in press).

Wolpin, M., and Pearsall, L. Rapid deconditioning of a fear of snakes. *Behavior Research and Therapy*, 1965, *3*, 107–111.

Wolpin, M., and Raines, J. Visual imagery, expected roles and extinction as possible factors in reducing fear of avoidance behavior. *Behavior Research and Therapy*, 1966, *4*, 25–37.

INDEX